THE ORIGINS OF THE ENGLISH
PEOPLE

> .... *syththan eastan hider*
> *Engle ond Seaxe*   *up becomen*
> *Ofer brad brimu,*   *Brytene sohten,*
> *Wlance wigsmithas*   *Wealas ofercomon,*
> *Eorlas arhwate*   *eard begeaton.*

> ....   since from the east hither
> Angles and Saxons   up did come,
> Over the broad sea's brim;   Britain they sought,
> Wise war-smiths,   the Welsh overcoming,
> Earls fame-loving,   and the land they seized.

From the Anglo-Saxon poem *The Battle of Brunnanburgh*

BERAM SAKLATVALA

THE ORIGINS OF THE ENGLISH PEOPLE

TAPLINGER PUBLISHING COMPANY
NEW YORK

First published in the United States in 1970 by
TAPLINGER PUBLISHING CO., INC.
29 East Tenth Street
New York, New York 10003

SBN 8008 - 6115 - 9

Library of Congress Catalog Card Number
70-85491

Printed in Great Britain

CONTENTS

LIST OF ILLUSTRATIONS

PLATES

All photographs not otherwise acknowledged are by courtesy of the Trustees of the British Museum

MAPS

VIKINGS

DANES

ANGLES

SAXONS

JUTES

NORTH SEA

Isle of Wight

Pevensey

NORMANS
(Settlement of Danes and Vikings)

THE INVADERS

PROLOGUE

FROM their tiny kingdom lying off the northern shores of Europe the Anglo-Saxon people went out over the world taking their laws, their methods of government, and their language with them. They built their colonies in North America, setting out their farms in the wide plains and green valleys of the New World. They peopled Australia and New Zealand. They went into Africa and into Asia—governing many different people to whom they taught their language and their law. They planted Parliaments in many lands, believing that representational government and government by consultation and consent were unarguably and self-evidently the best. Some of these Parliaments have thrived and some have changed into institutions far different from that at Westminster.

For three hundred years or more they dominated the oceans of the globe and for a brief hundred and fifty years they dominated the world itself. As Rome had dreamed of a world of free citizens, with people of many lands sharing a common law and a common loyalty, so did they dream, and briefly believed that the vision was reality. The fashion now is to deride the dream and to mock the dreamers of it. Yet the conception was not idle, nor completely unfulfilled. Through it, millions of folk around the world who are not kin to the Anglo-Saxon people have democracy as their ideal and the rule of law as their acknowledged aim.

The Anglo-Saxon people in their own kingdom, their blood and traditions enriched by their neighbours—the Scots, the Welsh and the Irish—have given much to the world, perhaps more than the world now cares to acknowledge. The same folk,

9

enriched by the adventurous and the poor, by the exiled defenders of lost causes, by the dispossessed and the persecuted, who
thronged to them from all the countries of Europe, have built a
younger and vigorous land in the New World.

Greece had great gifts to offer, but left to the Romans the
task of disseminating those gifts throughout the civilised world.
The Anglo-Saxon folk have been their own messengers. Rome
built the long roads along which Hellenistic thought travelled to
Asia Minor, North Africa, Spain and the Yorkshire moors. The
Anglo-Saxons built their own ships and their own roads by
which were transmitted their ideas of government by consent,
of freedom to worship God in any way a man pleases, and of a
body of law that binds all men—including kings and lawmakers.
For they have possessed through succeeding ages not only these
basic ideas on how society should be organised, but also a great
restlessness—the knowledge that the sea is a highway and not a
barrier, and the belief that a man may make a home wherever a
ship can carry him. A man can exercise his skills anywhere—can
rear sheep or raise cattle even though midsummer day blazes
in December, can fell a tropic thorn tree as well as a northern
oak, and can drive a plough in a vast field many thousand miles
westward of his former and smaller farm.

Where did the Anglo-Saxon people obtain these qualities?
Their impatience with authority, their obstinacy in defeat, their
insistence upon old and inalienable rights, their urge to build
new homesteads and new countries overseas—are all these
things inherited, and reinforced by a process of natural selection?
What were the different ethnic components that made up the
whole people, and what were the main events that brought together the many different folk who went to their making? These
are the matters which this book will explore.

I

THE FIRST ENGLISH

T HE island of Britain does not lie precisely north and
south but is tilted westward, so that the west coast of
Scotland reaches out towards the Atlantic ocean, its
peninsulas shattering into many rocky islands, rearing through
the moving waters. The east coast of Britain leans to the north-
west, growing ever further from the neighbouring lands across
the North Sea. In the south, however, the peninsula of Kent
stretches purposefully eastwards. At the North Foreland, on the
green fields that crown the low cliffs of white chalk, ochred with
yellow sand, a squat lighthouse guides sailors and fishermen to
the entrance of the English Channel. Beyond it lie the lonely
waters of the North Sea. Southward lies France, to be reached
in a brief journey. But eastward, as the land points, Germany
and Denmark are distant by many days sailing.

South of the North Foreland, Pegwell Bay sweeps inland. To
the north and west it is bounded by low white cliffs, that fall
away to flat beaches and low-lying land in the south. On a
summer's day, looking eastward, the far horizon and distant
sea can be as blue as a Mediterranean scene. Down by the sea's
edge at the centre of the bay, in the dry and pebbly sand above
the reach of high water, sparse grasses grow. A ridge of small
stones, built slowly by the patient tides, stands between the dry
grasses and the sea. In summer the water chuckles gently round
the pebble ridge; in autumn and winter it snarls over the stones,

reminding us of the grey waste beyond, the lonely path of whales in days gone by, leading through angry and bitter weather to the broken coast of north Germany.

It was in this bay, and up this pebble ridge, that three small ships brought the first English to the island of Britain, one and a half thousand years ago—probably in the year AD 446. Each ship would have carried some eighty to a hundred men. These

SAXON SHIP

two or three hundred barbarian soldiers—their hands hardened by long days of rowing, their backs stiff from the labour of the oar bench, their faces reddened by the sea winds, their hair and clothing salt-encrusted—these were the founders of the new nation of the English and of the many English-speaking lands that were to be built across even wider and deeper seas.

They had come a long and weary journey from the shores of Germany north of the mouth of the Elbe, four hundred miles from Pegwell Bay. No doubt they sailed close to the shore where they could, first westwards, with the Frisian Islands to starboard, then turning south to follow the flat coastline to the mouth of the Rhine. Thence they swung westwards again, along the coast of the Frankish lands, finally striking across the open sea to make landfall on the Kentish coast, and so into the sheltered waters of Pegwell Bay.

The three ships were curved at prow and stern, and along the low bulwarks were slung the men's shields making a brightly coloured defensive wall. On each ship the single mast carried a square sail so that they could make good speed in a following wind. But the long sea-oars and the hardened muscles of the men were the chief power of their sailing. The steersman leaned on the heavy tiller which turned the steering oar placed to one side near the stern—the steering side or 'stearbord', as it remained for many centuries, long after ship design had changed out of all recognition.

Long and weary had the journey been, but it was one to which these folk had been accustomed. For nearly two hundred years their forbears—and perhaps they themselves—had sailed these same seas in search of treasure and booty from the rich countryside of the decaying Roman Empire. Along the coast of Britain they had made their ruffianly landings, and the shores of Gaul had been misted by the smoke of their harrying. Sometimes they had landed small armies which marched inland to challenge the authority of the Romans or of the Britons. Their curved ships had become a byword among the sophisticated and civilised provincials, symbolising cruelty, ruthlessness and skill at sea.

They came now on a far different errand, not to attack and conquer but to defend and serve. As soldiers, under their leader Hengist, they were to help the Britons against the ravaging Picts from the northern parts of the island. For, as will be described in Chapter 3, the Britons who for four hundred years had been guarded by the three Roman legions stationed in the province were now stripped of their defences. The great masonry Wall built by the Emperor Hadrian in the first century, stretching majestically for some seventy-four miles from Wallsend-on-Tyne (four and a half miles east of Newcastle) to Bowness-on-Solway, was no longer garrisoned. Eighteen to twenty feet high, with forts spaced a mile apart (much of it is still visible today), it had for three hundred years protected the Roman province from the inroads of the Picts and Caledonians. But now the legions had departed and the Roman administration had fallen away. The land had split into many tribal kingdoms which had battled bravely against their numerous enemies. Finally, following Roman precedent, the most powerful king among them, Vortigern, enlisted these soldiers from Germany; in return for land, pay and supplies they were to fight on behalf of the Britons, against the northern barbarians. It was with this purpose, and with the promise of a permanent settlement in a new land, that the men hauled their three ships up the pebbled ridge, made them fast, and set foot in Britain.

Although we now believe that they were Jutes, in the earliest written records of these events the men are described as Saxons. Among the Britons, the monk Gildas wrote an account about a hundred years after this first landing, when the Britons and the Germanic invaders had turned to fighting one another fiercely for possession of the island. He knew that the newcomers were to mutiny, were to send for reinforcements from Germany, and ultimately were to wage savage war against his own people. With this hindsight he recorded that King Vortigern and his counsellors

> introduced these ferocious Saxons of unspeakable name, hateful to God and men, bringing as it were wolves into the fold in order to beat back the nations of the north . . . A flock of cubs burst forth from the lair of the barbaric lioness . . . They landed first in the eastern part of the island and there fixed their horrible claws, pretending that they were going to fight for our country, but really to fight against it.

As these men stepped ashore they were not merely stepping into a new land, but across the frontier that divides pre-history from history. West of the Rhine and in the island of Britain, the Roman Empire looked back over four hundred years of recorded history. But in the dark forests eastwards, and along the coast east of the Rhine estuary, the tribes of Germany fought and farmed, sailed and adventured, with no chroniclers to write their story. Even so, something is known of the kind of people they were.

Some three hundred and fifty years before the three ships came to Kent, the Roman author Tacitus (writing about AD 98) had made a close and detailed study of the tribes of Germany. He was moved to do so not only by the spirit of scientific enquiry; he had political motives as well. Highly critical of the imperial form of government which Rome had adopted, he looked back with regret to the old days of the Republic, when morals were purer and when the sovereign power was truly vested in the Senate and people of Rome, rather than in one man. So he praised the noble savages of Germany, contrasting them, by implication, with the ignoble and degenerate citizens of the Empire. Even so, most of what he wrote is factual and is the result of a careful collecting of information from many sources.

It is in his pages that the English people are first recorded, under their Latin names of the *Angli* or Angles. Tacitus lists them as one of the many tribes whose territories bordered on that of the Langobards. Their land was a wild one, guarded by rivers and wide forests. His statement that they worshipped an Earth goddess whom he calls 'Nerthus' is supported by the fact that in Scandinavia there was in later times a deity named *Njorthr*. Tacitus adds that there was a wood dedicated to the goddess on one of the islands in the ocean, implying that the Angles, as early as the first century, dwelt near the sea and were already a seafaring folk, with their holiest place on an island to which as a matter of course they sailed at their season of festival. Their form of worship was primitive and cruel : after a solemn procession in which the goddess Nerthus was drawn in a cart hauled by cows, the slaves attending her were drowned in a secret lake.

Among the tribes who were neighbours to the Angles, Tacitus names the *Eudoses*. There has been speculation as to whether these were the Jutes, one of the tribes that were later to become part of the Anglo-Saxon nation, and the tribe to which Hengist and his men almost certainly belonged. Though Tacitus says no more specifically about the Angles, he has a great deal of information about the customs of the tribes of Germany generally, which may be applied to the particular tribes considered here, giving a picture, however slight, of the ancestors of the English people. That his observations were accurate is borne out by the fact that some traces of what he describes can be noted in their later history and are still dimly to be seen in Anglo-Saxon societies, in England and elsewhere.

First Tacitus notes that the only historical records maintained among these people were old songs in which they celebrated the adventures of their gods. This was still true many centuries later when they were dwelling in Britain, and some part at least of their earlier history can be extracted, as we shall see, from the ancient songs that were later set down in writing and so preserved.

They were governed by kings, selected from men of noble birth, so that kingship among them was partly hereditary, partly elective. Later the same attitude can be seen persisting : for in the ninth century, Alfred the Great was elected King though he was not the direct heir but merely the brother of his dead predecessor, who had left a young son. Even in modern times, part of the British coronation ceremony consists of the showing of the new monarch to the lords and people and the seeking of their approval to his consecration. In 1936, a king was replaced by his brother and this appeared to be done by the selection of the people, or at least by that of their representatives. From the earliest times Kings of England have never been permitted to be monarchs absolute; they have always had to depend for their power upon the will of the people. When they ignore this they do so at their peril. The English in England and in the North American colonies have demonstrated the vigour with which this doctrine is held. Moreover, they have always had to govern by consultation. Tacitus states specifically that in Germany the

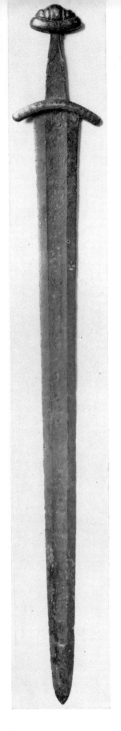

Page 17: (*left*) Anglo-Saxon sword; (*above right*) gold buckle with niello inlay, from Sutton Hoo. Suffolk, 7th century AD; (*below right*) Anglo-Saxon sword hilt.

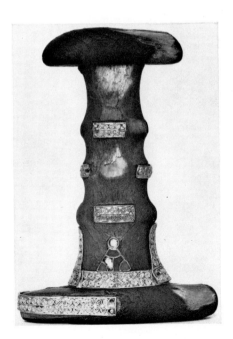

Page 18: Head, probably of the god Sulis, from Bath. This is Celtic work of the Roman period.

kings had neither unlimited nor arbitrary power. The elders or chiefs consulted together on all routine matters. Wider issues were discussed by all, but even these were first thoroughly considered by the chiefs. It would be fanciful to see in this practice a foreshadowing of debate in cabinet preceding debate in parliament, or of a president consulting his advisers before a general discussion by the people's representatives; but it is not fanciful to see enduring, through fifteen hundred years, a tradition of government by consultation.

The tribes' assemblies were far less formal than the Senate of Rome. They had, says Tacitus, no fixed times of meeting, and two or three days could be lost in calling all the men together. They came armed, and the assembly seems to have been very much a gathering of the fighting men. The priests called for silence and the first to be heard in debate would be the King, a chieftain or some other distinguished senior. Voting was by voice and acclamation. Again, it is perhaps fanciful to see a parallel with debates in the House of Commons, where proceedings begin with prayers by a priest, where the monarch's speech opens each session, where the monarch's ministers or former ministers are first to be heard in debate, and where all votes are initially taken by voice and acclamation. Parliament as we know it is less than a thousand years old. But the attitudes, aspirations and habits that formed it, and that required of government a continued dialogue between the executive and the people, are far more ancient.

There are closer likenesses between those assemblies of two thousand years ago and more modern institutions. For, according to Tacitus, it was before the council that accusations could be brought and men could be prosecuted for capital offences. The conception that law lay in the hands of a single man, the monarch, was not acceptable to English people. The law lay rather with the people themselves, and the assembly of the people was the ultimate arbiter. In this conception is perhaps a foreshadowing of the High Court of Parliament, of the judicial functions of the monarch's Privy Council, and of the setting up

B

of supreme courts in lands where the English people have moved entirely away from hereditary kingship, and have gone over completely to the principle of appointing their chiefs by election.

It was the assembly, too, that appointed a few selected men with local and delegated authority over the folk in their regions. The modern system of justices of the peace is not dissimilar. Tacitus tells little of the laws which governed these small societies, but includes a few significant details. Capital punishment was inflicted for a very limited number of offences. Hanging was reserved for traitors and deserters from the army. Men whom Tacitus refers to as 'cowards', and who were probably those who in times of war skulked at home, evading all service, were considered to be worse even than deserters; they were not hanged but buried alive in marsh or bog. The same punishment was awarded to homosexuals. For lesser crimes (including murder) the penalty was a fine. The infliction of the death penalty for numerous and frequently minor crimes in England during the eighteenth and nineteenth centuries seems to have been a temporary aberration, so that those who clamour for the reintroduction of the death penalty for murder are following national traditions less accurately than they themselves believe. The convicted man-slayer had to give so many horses or so many cattle —some to the king, representing the state, and some to the dead man's family. The same penalty was exacted for assault and wounding. This type of law persisted for many centuries and the schedules of fines for murder, the *wergeld* or 'man-money', are listed in the laws of the early kings in England, many centuries later. The suggestions recently advanced that criminals should compensate their victims from their prison earnings are in fact a strange echo of ancient practices.

Tacitus wrote more fully of the military organisation of these tribes. With the Romans, the military unit was the legion, to which men might be recruited from the ends of the earth, differing from one another in race, language and religion. They could have no natural or spontaneous loyalty; this had to be carefully and deliberately built, by discipline and by the ascription of almost supernatural powers to the standards, which every soldier had to protect and which each one came to worship. It was far otherwise among the tribes in Germany, where the unit was a detachment of a hundred men, coming from the same district and bound to one another by familiarity, friendship and kinship. In modern England both traditions endure. Units recruited for special duties follow the Roman pattern : the Royal Marines, the Royal Air Force, the Royal Artillery, like the legions are recruited from the whole country. But the units of infantry are drawn from the counties or, as the army is reduced, from groups of counties.

The German fighting men held a total and passionate devotion to their chief. It was this personal loyalty, sharper and more intense than any generalised patriotism, that gave their armies a terrible endurance in battle. It was the commander's duty to give an example of personal bravery; he considered it a disgrace to be outshone by any of his followers. They in turn were ashamed if their courage did not equal his; if the chief was killed on the field of battle it was considered a disgrace and dishonour for his followers to return alive. It was this that made them ultimately invincible; the disaster of a lost leader made them fight the harder and gave them the resolution to die where they stood. Defeat came only with the death of the last man, and at a bitter and often unacceptable cost to the enemy.

This particular tradition survived for centuries after the English came to Britain. In AD 755, three hundred years after their coming, the *Anglo-Saxon Chronicle* records an affray fought between King Cynewulf and Cyneheard, whom he was planning to drive out of his kingdom. Cyneheard surprised King Cynewulf at Merton where he had gone, with only a small bodyguard, to visit his mistress. Before the guard knew what was happening, Cyneheard's men beset the king in the lady's bower. The king rushed to the door, sword in hand, and fought alone against them all until he was killed. By this time the king's guard came running and saw their lord lying dead. Cyneheard called to them, and 'offered each of them money and life, and none of them would accept it, but they went on fighting continuously until they all lay slain, except one Welsh hostage, and he was badly wounded'.

Cyneheard's men seized the house and in the morning a party of the king's men rode up to the house and saw the dead king. Cyneheard came to the gates and offered them riches and land if they would give him the kingdom, but the king's men replied that 'no kinsman was dearer to them than their lord and they never would follow his slayer'. And they in turn told kinsmen of theirs who were with Cyneheard that they might go free. But these proudly answered that the same offer had been made to the men who had been with the king; and that they themselves could no more accept the offer than did those others who had been slain with Cynewulf. So in the grey morning they fought at the gate, the king's men forcing their way in against the shields and swords of their enemies, until they had killed Cyneheard and all his men save one only. Thus was the king's death avenged.

In this ruthless and bloody story there persists the tradition that loyalty to one's lord came before all other loyalties. With Cyneheard's men, it outweighed loyalty even to one's rightful king. It was greater than the ties of blood and kinship, than reason or logic; it bound all, of whatever party, to choose death rather than any kind of compromise or any chivalrous offer of safety.

Again, in AD 920, two hundred years later, and nearly five hundred years after the first English landed in Kent, the same tradition and the same proud seeking of death endured. In that year a battle was fought between the English and the invading Danes at Maldon in Essex and the tale was set down in a long poem (*The Battle of Maldon*) written at the time. It shows how the willingness to die when the chief was killed inevitably led to a larger result: great odds or the beginning of defeat became of no consequence. If the line were broken and many men wounded, if the enemy were stronger or more numerous—all this mattered not at all if the chief had not retreated or if he lay dead. For in the latter case death was the inevitable outcome of the warplay and the strength of the enemy was thus a total irrelevance.

At the battle of Maldon the leader of the English, Byrhtnoth, was wounded in the arm, so that his yellow-hilted sword fell to the earth, and he was hewn down by the Danes. A young soldier saw him fall and rallied the English line.

> Never among this people shall the thanes declare that I would fare forth away from this host and seek my home, now that my chief lies, cut down in the battle. To me this is the greatest of sorrows. He was both my kinsman as well as my lord.

So they fought on, man after man of them reminding his comrades of their duty and boasting grimly that he would never see home again now that his lord was dead. One by one they died, exacting from the Danes a terrible price for the victory. Since each man was resolved to die, and to move not one foot from the field, each in seeking death took more than one of the Danes with him. Finally, when few men were left alive, Byrtwold, one of the older men among the surviving English, called out to his friends in words that still sing:

> *Hige sceal the heardra, heorte the cenre,*
> *Mod sceal the mare, the ure maegen lythlath.*

> Thought shall be the harder, heart the keener,
> Mood shall be the more, as our might grows little.

In these lines may be seen a foreshadowing of Agincourt and Crécy, of Waterloo and the Battle of Britain. Unthinking loyalty to a lord or leader has long ceased to be an overriding motive with the English people. But to hold danger in scorn, odds in contempt, and retreat to be unthinkable; to see reasons for persisting in a struggle when all reason shouts aloud against its continuance; to realise that defeat is often a pause along the road to some unimagined victory; to know, after the spears have been thrown, after the arrows and missiles have done their work, that the shield-wall may be broken and that the final work must be man against man—all these things have perhaps endured.

Though their desperate courage even in a lost battle can stir men across the centuries, the motives and incentives that took these tribes to war were usually less romantic and less admirable. War for the tribes in Germany was not an instrument of policy as with the Romans. Nor were wars always fought in defence of a kingdom's rights and liberties. Tacitus notes that they were often engaged in merely for booty. A chief's standing was measured by the number of warriors who followed him. The men in his troop looked to him for their equipment and their keep. He provided them with horses, spears and food, and gave them the rings and other personal ornaments in which they delighted; but the gifts and equipment had to be won by the chiefs on the field of battle. Here again the words of Tacitus are supported by later and independent witnesses. In Anglo-Saxon poetry, written in England centuries after his day, the chief is often referred to as the giver of rings and the bestower of treasure. Indeed the word 'Lord' itself enshrines this same principle : in its original form it was *hlaford* or *loaf-giver*. Upon their lord the men of the troop depended for their very bread.

Wars for plunder and raids for booty would therefore have been frequent. Tacitus in a telling phrase records that this people considered it 'base and spiritless to gain by sweat what they might win by blood'. This is the way of all primitive and warlike tribes and too much should not be made of it. Yet the ghost of any one of Tacitus's warriors would not have felt himself an alien in the company of Sir Francis Drake or even of Captain Morgan; nor, if there is a Valhalla, will the ghosts of all those younger sons who for centuries have gone out of England to seek their fortunes in foreign wars find themselves out of sympathy with the shades of their remote ancestors.

Other minor matters would endorse their kinship. Tacitus records, for example, that the tribes in Germany counted periods of time by nights rather than by days; the English still call a period of two weeks a fortnight, dating from the time when it was conceived as a space of fourteen nights. And in Shakespeare's day a week was still a sennight or a space of seven nights. Even the favourite drink has been fairly constant : although the vine grows and flourishes in Germany, Tacitus notes that the drink of the tribesmen was a fermented liquid made from barley or wheat. He adds, with a touch of condescension, that the fermentation gave it a certain resemblance to wine ! Beer was clearly a novelty to him and made little appeal to his Mediterranean taste. He describes their food as simple—fruit, venison and curdled milk. Gambling was a frequent pastime : Tacitus found it extraordinary that, when they were sober, the tribesmen played at dice as if it had been a matter of serious business. They would stake all they had on the game, and would even bet their lives and liberties, going into willing slavery if they lost.

Although they lived together in villages, Tacitus notes that they did not plan these as the Romans did, with houses in neat rows; each man, when building his house, surrounded it with an open space. Tacitus ascribes this either to a sensible desire to reduce the risk of fire, or to an ignorance of architecture and building skills, but perhaps his urban eyes could not see the pleasure that a man takes in privacy and in a garden.

So some picture exists, however faint, of the Angles, Saxons and Jutes long before they came to Britain, of their attitudes and behaviour, in their peacetime assemblies and in their grim battle-lines, wielding ash spear and stout shield, wearing the rings and ornaments given them by their loved lord. In their island temple they worshipped the earth goddess; they ate simply and drank deeply, following their kings faithfully but impatient of any tyranny. This was the background of the men aboard the ships that sailed bravely into Pegwell Bay; and these were the beliefs and social patterns that they and those who came after them planted in their new lands.

The first of their kings whose actions were written down and have survived was Offa, who reigned while the tribes were still in Germany. His descendants came to Britain, became kings, and ruled over Mercia, the large kingdom stretching across the

Midlands. Alfred of Wessex married a princess of the house of Mercia; through her the present royal family of England is thus directly descended from Offa. As mentioned earlier, the Angles and Saxons for centuries celebrated the prowess of their heroes in poems sung in hall or camp, and what may be the oldest surviving English poem, *Widsith*, dates in part from the seventh century, some two hundred years after their coming to Britain. It records the deeds of many kings and that

> Offa ruled over Angel. Alewih ruled over the Danes and, though he was the bravest of men, he did not outdo Offa in his mighty deeds. Offa, best of men, won by force of arms, while he was still but a boy, the greatest of kingdoms. No one as young as he did braver deeds in battle with his own sword alone. He marked out a boundary against the Myrgingas at *Aegidor*. The Angli and the Suevi held it thereafter as Offa marked it out.

These terse and laconic lines tell much. Offa's golden reputation had shone for three centuries or more and had survived the migration of his people from the old lands of the Angles into the island of Britain. Moreover he achieved his greatest victory while he was still little more than a boy. There is a hint that this victory was won in single combat—with his own sword alone. Aegidor, the Door of Aegir, a great sea-monster, is the old name for the river Eider which runs westwards across the neck of the peninsula of Denmark. So Offa's victory was fought against an enemy who was attacking the Angles across that river, that is to say from the south. Because of Offa's victory the river Eider became the southern boundary of the Angles and remained so thereafter.

Who was this southern enemy?

Claudius Ptolemaeus (known as Ptolemy the Geographer), who lived at Alexandria in Egypt during the second century, lists in his geography the tribes of Germany, enumerating them from the west to the east. He notes that the Lesser Chauci extended as far as the river Weser; then came the Greater Chauci as far as the river Elbe; 'then, upon the neck of the Cimbric Peninsula, the Saxons'. Ptolemy's Cimbric Peninsula is the modern Denmark, so his words place the Saxons between the Elbe and the Eider, precisely in the area from which Offa's enemies attacked. We shall see that later tradition does indeed describe Offa's antagonist as a Saxon.

Offa's reign is also recorded in another poem, *Beowulf*, a later composition than *Widsith* and probably written down about AD 700. It tells how Beowulf, a great hero and a thane of King Hygelac of the Goths, sailed with fourteen companions to the land of the Danes where King Hrothgar had for twelve years been plagued by the foul monster Grendel; Beowulf, of course, finally slew Grendel after many adventures. The poem is part history and part legend, and since the setting is in the kingdom of the Danes (the Cimbric Peninsula), it is not surprising that, like *Widsith*, it embodies something of the traditions of the Angles and a brief reference to the famous Offa :

> Offa, as I have heard, a chief of heroes, was the best of all men of the earth who dwell between the seas. For Offa was a brave man among the spears, and widely renowned for his generous giving and for his victories. He wisely ruled his own land. From him was descended Geomar, support of the warriors, kin to Hemming, and of the line of Garmund, mighty in war.

King Offa was therefore remembered not only as a hero, a brave man among the spears, but as a generous and open-handed leader of the kind described by Tacitus—one who provided his troop of men with their horses, spears and armour; centuries after his death his munificence was still recalled. Moreover, the tradition embodied in *Beowulf* suggests that he was celebrated as a wise leader in peace as well as a victorious leader in battle. It further records the names of one of his descendants, Geomar, and of one of his ancestors Garmund, both of whom are found in another document (their names modified to Eomaer and Waermund). The traditions brought to England by the Angles from Germany indeed record something of the genealogy of their past kings as well as the names and isolated deeds of ancient heroes.

Some time in the ninth century, in the English kingdom of Mercia, men wrote down the pedigree of their kings, ending it with the name of King Aethelred. In the *Anglo-Saxon Chronicle* under the date AD 704, this Aethelred, son of Penda, is recorded as renouncing the throne of Mercia and becoming a monk. 'He had held the kingdom twenty-nine winters'; thus he had become king in AD 675, the date also given by Bede. The ninth-century pedigree traces Aethelred's ancestry right back to the mythical Woden, and Offa's name appears nine generations before Aethelred's. Taking three kings to the century, this gives Offa's date as some time in the late fourth century. He must therefore have been reigning at the time when Roman rule was beginning to crumble in Britain, and rumours of events there may well have reached him in his German kingdom. Men from his land may have taken the opportunity to sail across the North Sea in search of booty and adventure, fighting and plundering on the Roman island. Almost certainly men from the neighbouring kingdom of the Saxons did so at that time.

Some eighty years later the three ships came to Pegwell Bay. For the soldiers they carried, coming from lands near to Offa's own, Offa's battle would have been about as familiar as are the battles of Mons and Ypres to Britons today; men were still living who had witnessed the action, and the tale was told and retold in camp and hall. The fame of Offa's prowess also lingered on in the lands near the old Angle kingdom. Some eight centuries after the Angles had settled in their new country of England, two writers in Denmark recorded Offa's great victory. Although so late in date, these stories are significant, for they represent the traditions that had been handed down in the original lands of the Angles. The versions brought to Britain in the fifth and sixth centuries would have suffered change and embellishment during the succeeding years; in Denmark the same stories would have undergone the same kind of process, but the changes would have been different, so that the two traditions began to diverge. Assuming that there was no continued contact beween the two countries, whatever is common to both the English and the

Danish versions may well be based on the original narrative as it stood in the fifth and sixth centuries—before the separation of the two traditions; and it may therefore contain something of the facts of the story.

One of the Danish writers, Saxo Grammaticus (writing some time after AD 1200) includes the same basic elements that are given in the English poems—telling of a battle on the river Eider against an enemy from the south, and introducing Offa (here named Uffo) as the son of Wermund, thus supporting the evidence of *Beowulf*. These points may therefore be taken as factual. How much of the rest of the story is built up from the encrustations of centuries cannot be known, but many of the details have some ring of truth. Saxo Grammaticus writes that King Wermund grew old and blind, and the King of the Saxons demanded that he should give up his kingdom, challenging Wermund that the matter should be settled by single combat between the two kings' sons. The King of the Saxons had a brave and able son; King Wermund's son Uffo was tall and powerful but dull-witted and totally dumb. Wermund had therefore to reject the challenge; instead, blind as he was, he proposed that he himself should fight the young prince of the Saxons. The Saxon heralds scornfully rejected Wermund's offer and the old king was in despair. Suddenly Uffo regained the power of speech and said that he would accept the challenge and fight for his father's kingdom. He would fight not merely the son of the Saxon king, but also any companion whom that prince might bring.

So Uffo had to be equipped for the fight, but no sword could be found strong enough for his powerful arm. Then Wermund sought out his old sword Skrep which he had used in his youth, and which he had buried away thinking he had no son worthy to wield it. With this and a shield Uffo strode alone to the place chosen, an island 'encircled by the waters of the river Eider'. Thither too went the Saxon prince, but attended by a companion famous for his prowess. Crowds thronged the banks to see the battle upon which the freedom and destiny of the Angles depended. Wermund stood at one end of a bridge, to follow the sounds of the struggle and, despite his blindness, to learn the fate of his kingdom. He had little hope that his dullard son would conquer and had determined to leap into the river and drown once the battle had been lost.

At first Uffo struck no blow, but was content to guard himself with the shield, sizing up his adversaries. King Wermund's despair increased and he left the bridge, moving nearer to the water's edge. Then Uffo taunted the prince's companion and goaded him to come and fight more closely. Raising his sword, Uffo now struck his first blow, splitting his adversary in two. The blind Wermund heard the blow with joy and one of his followers described to him what had happened. He moved from the shore back to the bridge, now filled with hope. And finally he heard the sound of Skrep for the second time, as Uffo dealt the Saxon prince his death blow. So the kingdom of the Angles was saved and the river Eider, as *Widsith* recorded and as is described earlier by Ptolemy, was confirmed as the permanent boundary between the continental kingdoms of the Angles and the Saxons.

The other Danish writer, Sweyn Aageson (whose work is of earlier date, before AD 1200), adds one detail to explain why Uffo, though challenged to single combat, offered to fight two of the Saxons. Years earlier two Angles whose father had been killed together avenged his death upon the murderer. This breach of the laws of honour had so shocked Uffo that he became dumb; it was to wipe out this disgrace that he now reversed the odds.

It is a strange irony that the first recorded action of the Angles is a battle against the Saxons. These two nations (who were later to merge as the Anglo-Saxon people and who were together to settle in so many wild lands) are thus first seen as adversaries, eyeing one another with jealous hostility across the flowing waters of a wide river—and no doubt trading with each other in the peaceful intervals. The story illuminates much of what followed. War does not merely divide nations; it brings them into close contact, so that warring peoples often learn from one another and move into an intimate relationship. Some fifty years after Offa's death, when the first Saxons came to Britain, the separate identities of the two peoples were already blurred : to the Celtic and Roman inhabitants of the island, all were Saxons. The same confusion continued after they had settled in Britain. King Penda of Mercia (who died about AD 650) was a direct descendant of Offa and thus an Angle of proud and royal lineage; nevertheless in the *Annals of Tigernach*, a Welsh chronicle, he is described as 'Panta the Saxon'. Perhaps once Offa's sword had marked out a clear and permanent boundary between the two kingdoms, old hostilities had faded and the two nations had become allies, helping each other against common enemies.

A very early British writer, Nennius, whose *History of the Britons* was compiled about AD 800, describes the men in the three ships as Saxons. Yet later in the same account their elders are described as of the 'Oghgul' race—which may well mean that Nennius believed that they were Angles. What is absolutely clear from later events is that after the first settlers came to Britain, and when they sent for reinforcements from Germany, Angles and Saxons alike sailed for Britain, carving out their separate kingdoms not at first as enemies but as joint adventurers and joint exploiters of the rich lands of the province. Nor, when wars broke out between the kingdoms, was there any particular predisposition for Saxon to fight Angle. Angle fought Angle and Saxon strove against Saxon as readily and greedily, and for the same motives—lust for power and for land—as had brought the two nations to oppose one another. Arriving as friends if not as allies, they appear to have quarrelled over the spoils of war and the division of territory, and finally to have come together as one people, naturally and almost indistinguishably. Bede, writing in the eighth century, three hundred years after the first settlements, was a man of scholarly precision; he was the first to name the separate races of Angles, Saxons and Jutes as being the first invaders. Yet in his *Ecclesiastical History of the English People* he refers to the invaders of Kent as the 'nation of the Angles or of the Saxons'. He saw them as virtually one people, and as having been virtually so when first they landed.

The earliest actions of the Saxons themselves are less well documented than those of the Angles. Tacitus is silent about them; indeed, from the evidence of continental writers we should never know that the Saxons were among those who left Germany to settle in Britain. Yet, by the end of the fourth century, it is they who were seen by the citizens of the Roman Empire as foremost among the raiding German tribes and it is their name which the early chroniclers exclusively use.

The first mention of the Saxons as raiders is in the pages of Eutropius, who was writing between AD 364 and 378—the dates of the Emperor Valens to whom he dedicated his *Epitome of Roman History*. He describes how the Romans appointed Carausius to guard the seas off the coast of northern France, which the Franks and Saxons were pillaging. A few years later Ammianus Marcellinus also wrote a history of Rome, and reports that about AD 365 the Picts, Saxons, Scots and Attacotti were causing trouble in Britain. This was about the period of Offa's reign, some eighty years before the Saxon settlers arrived in Britain, so that some at least of Offa's father's enemies, against whom he fought, could have told him tales of the land where his descendants were to reign. It is Ammianus who notes that the Saxons were feared above all other enemies of the Empire because of the unexpected swiftness of their raids. They must, however, have ceased to harass Britain for at least some years before King Vortigern recruited them as allies.

What did those first Germanic soldiers find when they landed in Kent? What kind of people inhabited the country and how were they organised? How did the Angles and Saxons come to seize the land for themselves? What factors changed them, so that their descendants—the Anglo-Saxon people of the modern world—have a character and traditions similar to but at the same time different from those of Germany whence they came? Did they displace or slaughter the Celtic and Roman inhabitants of the land of Britain, setting up purely Germanic kingdoms? Or did their seed mingle with that of the older people of the island? Is there indeed an Anglo-Saxon race, as politicians infer, or is there rather an Anglo-Celtic people which shares the heritage of two distinct folk?

II

CELTS, ROMANS AND SETTLERS

THOUGH the Roman civilisation was crumbling when the first English arrived in Britain, much of its material apparatus still stood. At either end of the Isle of Thanet where they landed, there loomed up on the Kentish shore the forbidding grey walls of a major Roman fort. To the south stood Portus Rutupiae, the modern Richborough; its tall stone walls, with bonding courses of red brick, stood foursquare on the high land above the entrance to the channel. Massive bastions added to their menace, and upon these were the platforms where the great Roman war engines had once been placed. Within the walls, red roofs crowded round a huge central monument, marble-faced and gleaming white in the northern light. This monument (its plinth is still standing) bore a proud inscription and was one of Britain's landmarks. For it was here, four hundred years earlier, that the legions of Claudius had first landed for the conquest of the island; and it was from this spot that the Roman power had gradually spread northwards and westwards into the tribal lands to create an orderly and prosperous province.

From the towering western gateway of the old fort the Roman road ran inland to the walled city of London, where it turned north-westward. Through towns and villages, past government stables where once changes of horses were kept ready for travellers, over plains and rolling hills, across green valleys and dark

Page 35: Tombstone from Chester of Caecilius Avitus, a junior officer (*optis*) of the Twentieth Legion. He was born at Emerita Augusta (the modern Mérida) in Spain and died in Britain at the age of thirty-four.

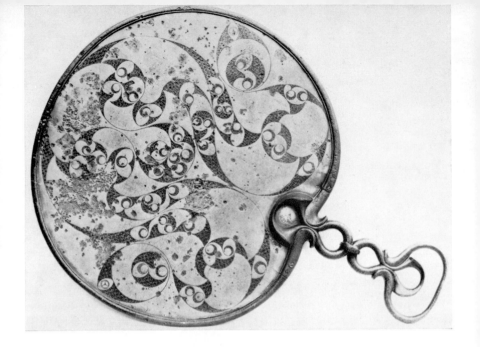

Page 36: (*above*) British bronze hand mirror with curvilinear decoration, from Desborough, Northamptonshire, 1st century AD ; (*below*) British decorated pot showing chariot and horses.

forests, the road ran straight and purposeful to the city of Chester which until recently had been garrisoned by the Twentieth Legion. On the roofs of the now deserted barracks the tiles still displayed the rampant boar, the legion's badge.

York, the military capital of the north, Lincoln, which stood at the centre of miles of farmland once allotted among retired legionaries, Bath, with its temple to the god Sulis, whose sun-rayed face still gazed from the pediment, Winchester, Exeter, Colchester—all these cities remained, and were still linked by Roman roads which, though now falling into disrepair, remained serviceable. They could still carry an army deep into the four corners of the province, as they had been planned and built to do. Devised by the Romans for pacification and defence, the road system could now serve as a means of attack and occupation.

The cities, though shabby, were not deserted. There were still magistrates and prefects, tribunes and consuls; but they were men whose effective powers were far less than their titles suggested. The once trim shops were shabby and empty; trade was dying and money disregarded. Outside the walls of Chester, St Albans and other towns, stood fine theatres, gay with columns and with marble. But the actors had left the silent stages and the musicians had ceased to play for the summer dancers. Now men came there only to dump their broken pots and rubbish; and the town's refuse covered the floor of the orchestra and gathered knee-deep between the rows of seats.

Outside the cities, well-placed in sheltered valleys or in the fertile cornland, stood the villas. These were more than lux-uriously appointed country houses, centrally heated, with painted walls and ceilings and richly coloured mosaic floors. They were centres of agriculturally based industries, where leather was tanned, wool was spun and woven, and corn was stored in dry granaries. Here, where men were closer to the soil, less depend-ent than their brothers in the decaying cities upon man-made order and man-made trade, the corn still ripened, the sheep still grew their fleece against December's chill, and the sleek cattle

C

still prospered. If the cities reeked of dust and untended drains, of damp decay and crumbling plaster, the farms were little changed.

The people who tilled the farms and who still lived in the walled cities were a mixed folk of many origins. Basically the population was Celtic; but on to this stock many scions had already been grafted.

Britain first crossed the threshold of history in 55 BC when Julius Caesar led the first, and unsuccessful, Roman expeditionary force into the island from northern France. On this first occasion he achieved little and withdrew after a brief campaign. He therefore invaded the island a second time in the following year with more massive forces. When he later wrote his memoirs, in the form of a long commentary upon all his campaigns in both foreign and civil wars, Caesar dealt with his two invasions of Britain in some detail, and so for the first time Britain and her people came under the scrutiny of a trained and literate observer who recorded much of what he saw for himself, and much of what he learned from his agents and observers.

As a soldier, for the most part he recorded points of purely military interest. But from these scant and tersely expressed items of information much may be deduced. For example, while he was still assembling his army in northern France and moving his troops to their embarkation points, delegates approached him from many of the tribes of Britain : they had heard of his intentions, and came to offer submission to the Roman power, thus hoping to avoid the blood and torment of an armed invasion. That news of the planned invasion reached the island so swiftly, and that delegates were able to visit Caesar promptly in his headquarters, shows that the people of Britain—or at any rate those in the south—had close contact with Gaul. These contacts were no doubt based upon an abundant cross-channel trade, the most likely stimulus to sea-travel. It is also clear that although society in the island was tribal, with no central or paramount authority, the tribes (again in the south-east) were accustomed to consult together and to act in concert when circumstances required. Without some pre-existing means of consultation they could not have organised the peace mission to Caesar swiftly enough to reach him before he sailed, nor could that mission have comprised representatives from several of the tribes, bringing a unified and comprehensive proposal.

Caesar also recorded that the form of government was monarchical, each tribe having its own king, and that wars and rivalries arose between the different kingdoms. The Trinovantes (who dwelt in what is now Essex) had been attacked by King Cassivelaunus whose territories lay around Wheathampsted and St Albans. He had slain the king of the Trinovantes, whose son fled to Caesar for protection.

That external danger was no new experience for the Britons emerges obliquely from Caesar's memoirs. Writing of the fighting on the beaches during his first expedition, he mentions that the Britons drove their horses into the sea to fight the Roman troops immediately they leapt from the ships; he adds significantly that the horses were specially trained for this type of action. Moreover the cavalry did not fight at random nor without a plan. Later in the battle, the mounted Britons waited on the high ground above the beach until they saw that a few Roman soldiers had disembarked and were wading ashore. They then urged their horses into the shallows and surrounded the Romans as they tried to reach dry land. These practised tactics used to oppose an armed landing, and the Britons' intimate knowledge of the shallows, suggest that raids from the Continent were frequent enough for the Britons to have been compelled to develop and perfect the defences of their island. Not only commerce but war had launched many ships over the tumbling waters of the Channel before Caesar's vast fleet swept into attack.

The population of the areas he visited appeared large to Caesar, and he is fairly informative on the inhabitants' level of civilisation. The countryside was densely built over, the houses resembling those of Gaul. Cattle were numerous and the land rich and prosperous. Tin and iron were both worked, and bars of iron of standard weight were used as currency, though gold coins were also produced; bronze had to be imported. According to Strabo, writing in the time of Caesar's successor, Augustus, the Britons exported to the continent gold, silver, iron, cattle and hunting dogs, slaves and corn. Caesar noticed an inequality between the cultures of the different regions: Kent was by far the most civilised, its standards being indistinguishable from those of Gaul. Some of Caesar's apparent contradictions may be explained by these regional differences. For example he recorded that most of the tribes of the interior did not grow corn but lived on meat and milk, yet tells of extensive cornfields and describes how the Seventh Legion was ambushed while out of camp foraging for corn. He also describes the existence of a form of group marriage, with ten or twelve men (often brothers) having a number of wives in common. He may have observed this in some of the more primitive and probably pre-Celtic tribes.

The Britons themselves recognised the various origins of the different tribes. According to their traditions the people near the coast were descended from immigrants from Gaul, who had first come to plunder and who had remained as settlers. Archaeology now supports the reliability of the tradition and of Caesar's recording of it. This pattern of population flow is to be expected in an island, and was indeed the pattern to be followed by the Anglo-Saxons. Over the long centuries wave after wave of people had crossed from the continent to seek land in the fertile island of Britain. Remembrance of this had perhaps made the coastal people, themselves the descendants of invaders, particularly vigilant against dispossession by others. These traditions, as well as more recent events, explain the carefully planned shore defences, with a mobile army following on land the path of Caesar's ships; and explain also the special training of the horses which, heads tossing and manes streaming in the salt wind, strode out through the sandy waters with the foam lapping their fetlocks on that terrifying summer day when the sea was crowded with strange ships disgorging armoured men.

Cultures and races overlapped. In some areas a primitive form of totemism appears to have survived; for Caesar reports that geese, cocks and hares were considered sacred and were not eaten. Yet in other districts society was highly organised and sophisticated. When King Cassivelaunus abandoned all hope of defeating the Romans in formal battles, he adopted guerrilla

BRITISH POT (CASTOR WARE) WITH SLIP DECORATION OF
RUNNING HARES

tactics and dismissed the greater part of his army. But he kept with him about four thousand charioteers. To equip and maintain this number of charioteers, all with highly trained teams of horses and with a full supply of weapons, argues a rich and well-organised kingdom. The original host had been far larger and gives a measure of the degree of organisation within the tribal kingdoms.

In battle the Britons were brave but volatile. Caesar describes them as quick to recognise defeat and to make peace; but quick to resume fighting when the time seemed favourable. They had all the bravery of the Angles and Saxons who were to take over their island; they had perhaps more dash and spirit in attack. But they lacked the tenacity in defence and the inability to recognise defeat that marked the men from Germany. They fought without armour but had a highly developed cavalry, their chariots being swift and magnificently handled; the tactics and skill of the charioteers showed a high degree of specialisation and training.

Strabo reported that the men were darker than the Gauls. They were also taller, but less well-built and less straight of limb. Caesar adds that they grew their hair long and wore moustaches; and that, as every schoolboy knows, they used woad as a blue warpaint.

Their art was well-developed and highly distinctive, notable for two particular characteristics. First is the love of the curved line and of the circle. Abstract patterns made up of intersecting arcs are to be found on mirrors and shields of the period. Though derived from leaf scrolls or other natural objects, they represent nothing and depict nothing, being flowing patterns of line, not even precisely symmetrical. But they have a rhythm and symmetry of their own, holding much in common with music—the same freedom from the oppression of the real world, the same timeless quality, and the same inevitable flow of phrase and shape. Second, when a natural object had to be depicted, it was shown in a formalised manner as if the artist preferred to keep close to his pure ideas of curvilinear pattern rather than to the duller task of accurate representation. The horses that appear in white slip on their pottery are elongated beasts, full of speed and curved energy, beasts from a withdrawn dream world into which the shagginess and muscularity of real horses never intrude. The White Horse of Uffington, on the Berkshire Downs, still shows something of the skill and vision of the abstract artists who carved it in the springy turf of the hillside, to stand perpetually as their memorial. The human face, too, in the hands of early British artists lacked the realism of the classical world. It became a brooding pattern of dreams, the eyes enlarged, the shape of the face changed to the shape of a mood, and the hair a stylised rhythm of interlocking lines. The face of the sun god Sulis at Bath shows how this tradition persisted through the Roman period, withstanding successfully the pressures of classical influence. Indeed something of it may perhaps be seen in taste and design within the island even to this day.

The conquering Romans were utterly different: fixed of

CELTIC SHIELD

purpose where the Britons were volatile; realists where they were imaginative and sensitive; masters of the setpiece battle where they were skilled in guerrilla warfare; concrete and representational in art where they were abstract and unreal; rectangular and rectilinear in designs and planning where they were curvilinear and rhythmic. For four hundred years the Britons lived under the stern discipline of Rome. Straight roads were built across their island, and neat towns with rectangular blocks and gridiron patterns of streets were built in the old tribal kingdoms. Kings gave way to prefects and magistrates. From Hadrian's

Wall to the Channel coast the land became one country, divided
into provinces with an orderly and precise hierarchy of government. And the Britons learned much. They learned about
national unity and the disciplines of war. They learned how to
use the wheeled plough and engines of war, how to build fortified places and roads and walled cities. But more enduring was
the enrichment of native blood and character by the descendants
of legionaries who settled in Britain.

At the time that Britain was finally conquered by the armies
of the Emperor Claudius (in AD 43), only Roman citizens were
permitted to enlist in the legions; to serve with the eagles was
a proud privilege granted only to free-born Romans. So the men
who marched in the ranks of the four legions that came to
conquer the island were Italian born, their mother tongue was
Latin and their ways and their culture were Mediterranean.
Their sojourn in Britain did not end with the campaign upon
which they came. Their units were stationed permanently in the
various provinces of the Empire. There were no trooping seasons
and no home leave. Three of the legions that conquered Britain
remained there for almost the entire period of the occupation.
Moreover, when the individual legionary had served his time
with the standards, he usually retired in the province where he
had been stationed. Rome's purpose was to ensure that there
were ex-soldiers available to help in times of emergency, and in
peacetime to furnish examples of discipline and civilisation to
their native neighbours. So the men who came from Italy, wor-
shipping different gods, lived with the Britons in harmony and
friendship, retaining their loyalty to Rome but developing a new
local loyalty to the land of Britain.

The process began early. Within twenty years of the conquest
a colony of ex-servicemen was living at Colchester in Essex.
Later, there were other colonies around Gloucester and Lincoln.
Some of the field boundaries of England may still follow the
lines set out by the Roman authorities when they allocated
rectangular plots of land to the ex-legionaries, the areas of whose
farms were calculated in proportion to their rank and their years

of service. The sons and daughters of the legionaries grew up on these farms as Britons, taking wives and husbands from among their Celtic neighbours. Many Britons, by the end of the Roman occupation, could boast of a Roman ancestor.

But it was not merely the blood of Italy that came to diversify the native population. Service in the legions ceased, in time, to be a privilege reserved for men of Roman birth, becoming instead a means whereby provincials and foreigners could win the proud honour of Roman citizenship. Men who were born in the remoter provinces, or indeed beyond the frontiers of the Empire, could now enlist. After serving with the eagles for the prescribed number of years, they were rewarded with Roman citizenship, with the right to contract a legal marriage, and sometimes with the grant of land in the province in which they had served. Gradually, therefore, the veterans who farmed in Britain included more and more men from lands other than Italy. These were men who had enlisted in the army, who had been posted to one of the three legions in Britain, who had served their time in the island, and who had finally been given honourable discharge and settled permanently in the land of their adoption.

There is good surviving evidence of the diverse origins of some of the soldiers in the legions. Chester was the garrison town of the Twentieth Legion, which because of its triumph over Queen Boudicca in AD 61 was given the proud title of the Victorious. Many of the men lie buried in the city where they had served. Some of their tombstones survive, carved with their names, their years of service, and in some cases the name of the land where they were born. Their origins include the most distant parts of the Empire.

The most senior officer whose tombstone has been found was Marcus Aurelius Alexander. He had probably taken his name from the Emperor who flourished in the middle-to-late third century, and this indicates a date for the stone. He had attained the high rank of camp prefect, which meant that he was second in command of his legion. Aged seventy-two when he died, he had no doubt long ended his active service, a reminder that many of the men who served in the legions in Britain never returned to their homeland. His epitaph records that he was born in Osroene, which is in Syria, then many months' journey from Britain.

At least one other soldier came from Syria and another from the Aegean shore of what is now Turlag. Others came from Thrace in northern Greece close to the Bulgarian border. One of the Thracians, Gaius Calventius Celer, must have died in Britain very early on in the occupation, for he was a soldier of the Second Legion which was stationed only briefly in Chester, from AD 80 to AD 86. Three of the men came from Spain. From Emerita Augusta, the modern Mérida, came Caecilius Avitus who had drawn his soldier's pay for fifteen years, and who died aged thirty-four, with the rank of *optio*, a junior non-commissioned officer. Maybe he served in the regimental office, for he is shown carrying two writing tablets. From the same town came Gaius Lovesius who enlisted when he was seventeen and died eight years later. Flavius Longus, a Tribune of the Twelfth Legion, came from Samosata on the Euphrates, and men came from Arles, Lyons and Fréjus in France, from Noricum, from Turin and Cremona, and from many other places.

Tombstones from Colchester tell a similar story. There is, for instance, Marcus Favonius Facilis, a centurion of the Twentieth Legion, who was the son of Marcus of the Pollian tribe— believed to have been one of the peoples of Italy. He may well have been born in Britain, since it is his father's origin and not his own which is recorded. If so, then he was typical of the increasingly cosmopolitan population of the island. That his father had been a member of a tribe in Italy was a fact worthy of mention, but he himself, born far from the vineyards and cypress trees of Italy, living and dying in the Northern province, needed no such identification. It was enough to record that here lay the body of a centurion of the Twentieth. The soil of Britain lay light over the remains of many Italian soldiers. Also from Colchester comes the tombstone of Longinus, an officer in the

First Squadron of Thracian cavalry, who came from Sardica, the modern Sofia in Bulgaria.

Some of course, came into the Roman province from nearer lands. From Colchester (and now in the British Museum) is a stone dedicated by Lossio Veda to Mars, the god of war. In the inscription Lossio Veda is described as the grandson of Vepogenus, a Caledonian; the reference to his grandfather suggests that his father had already settled in the Roman province before him. Thus blood from the northern tribes was already mingling with the blood of the Britons; not all the men who, in Roman times, marched south over Hadrian's Wall came on foray as hostile raiders : some, it appears, came to serve with the eagles.

Bath Museum has three tombstones recording the deaths of settlers from abroad. Lucius Vitellius Tancinus was a cavalryman serving in a squadron in Britain, and was the son of a Spaniard; the father of Peregrinus came from the tribe of the Treveri who gave their name to the city of Trèves; Priscus was the son of a stone-cutter, a citizen of the Carnutes tribe who gave their name to Chartres and lived near the site of the modern city. From the barracks and forts of Hadrian's Wall and many other places have come the names of foreign soldiers who travelled from afar to serve with the legions in Britain. Some are described on their tombstones as *missus honeste missione*, 'honourably discharged'; again, they had served their full time with the legions, had remained in Britain and had died there, having become part of the island's people. But it was not only the army that brought strangers into Britain. One of the memorial stones in Chester is dedicated to Flavius Callimorphus, aged forty-two, and to his little son Serapion who died when only three years old. Callimorphus is a Greek name, while Serapion seems to have been named after Serapis, one of the gods of Egypt. The family may well have been one of Greek traders from Egypt; they appear to have settled in Britain, for the tombstone was set up by Callimorphus' brother Theseus. Links with the people of the Nile are shown yet more clearly by an earthenware jug from

Southwark upon which are inscribed the words *Londini ad
fanum Isidis*—'At London, in the Temple of Isis'. So sometime
during the Roman occupation there was in London a shrine to
Isis, the Egyptian goddess. No doubt it was men from Egypt
who brought this cult to Britain. That a temple was built suggests
that at one time there may have been a permanent population
of Egyptians in London, and that they or their converts formed
a substantial group.

The god Mithras was also worshipped in London, almost
certainly on more than one site. This fact hints that soldiers
from overseas were stationed in the city, for Mithraism, whose
roots lay in Persia, was essentially a cult of the army; it did not
necessarily come to Britain directly from Persia. But the size and
cost of the Mithraic temple in London attest a numerous following; as London was not a town with a large garrison (it finds no
mention in the official list of Roman military centres) but a city
of commerce and trade, its adherents may have been drawn in
part from the city's cosmopolitan civilian population, or from
ex-servicemen who settled there. The goddess Atys, who came
from Phrygia (the modern Turkey), was another deity known
in London, and is further witness to the new ideas and new
people introduced during the occupation. The London Museum
has a fine memorial stone showing a nude boy standing and a
seated woman in a mourning attitude; inscribed in Greek : 'Good
Dexios, son of Diotimos, farewell', it is firm evidence for a Greek
family settled in the city. Traders, legionaries and officials from
all corners of the known world were arriving.

The process was a continuous one. Towards the end of the
period, a mere hundred years before the coming of the Saxons,
the legalisation of the new religion of Christianity gave a fresh
stimulus to travel and to the movement of people. Bishops from
Britain attended conferences in Gaul. Britons travelled to Rome,
to North Africa and to Greece. A Governor of Britain became
a bishop in Constantinople. The Celtic people of the island not
only became mixed in race, but grew aware of the wide world
that lay over their surrounding seas, and were conscious of being

part of a larger community of people and of ideas.

The contribution made by the army to this process was not merely through the individual soldiers. For Rome also had specialist units recruited entirely from men from distant lands. The Roman soldier was an expert in the use of the *pilum* and *gladium*—the javelin and the short sword. He was a superbly trained infantryman, magnificently disciplined, capable of long and rapid marches and of precisely executed manoeuvres on the field of battle. But he was less skilled as a cavalryman, and still less an expert in the use of the bow or the sling. The Roman authorities did not attempt to increase the versatility of the individual soldier, but recruited men from the subject races, or from the peoples outside the Empire, into special units using the particular weapons in which the men had a native skill. Thus in addition to the individual foreigners serving in the ranks, there were detachments of auxiliaries in which all the men came from the same country.

Many such units were stationed in Britain and their existence is well attested. Again, some of the evidence is to be found on the tombstones that once marked the graves of auxiliary troops who served and died in the island province; but the most complete and detailed account of the auxiliary detachments stationed in Britain is to be found in the *Notitia Dignitatum*—the list maintained by the Roman government of all the official appointments, both civil and military, throughout the Empire. Transcripts have survived of one of these lists, probably that for AD 428. It probably records the situation in Britain some thirty years earlier, towards the end of Roman rule. By that time numerous detachments of troops from overseas, cavalry and infantry, were in the forts and barracks of the province. There was a unit of the Nervii from Gaul and of Dalmatians from what is now Yugoslavia; along Hadrian's Wall were stationed Batavians and Tungrians; cohorts of men had come from Thrace and from Gaul.

Finally, the Roman authorities began the practice of enlisting entire tribes, each forming a self-contained unit, with their own chieftains or kings enrolled as Roman officers and exercising command. Such troops were removed from their native land (where often they had been hostile to the Roman power) and transplanted to new homes in another province. There they were given grants of land and so came to have a vested interest in the defence of their new area. In this way many new folk came into Britain—not all from overseas. About a hundred years before Hengist's ships sailed into Pegwell Bay, Constans (one of the sons of Constantine the Great and Emperor between AD 337 and 350) had brought into the province a group of Picts from the high hills of Caledonia, north of the Wall. These men would have been brought far to the south so that their new loyalties to Rome might be reinforced by long distance from their friends and the wild scenes of their former feuds and forays. Thus to the descendants of Greeks, Tungrians, Spaniards, Italians, Syrians and others were added the children of the Pictish soldiers. Constans also brought over from Ireland a group of soldiers from the tribe of the Scots, planting them in what is now Wales.

Similarly, some fifty years later, in the reign of Valentinian I, a whole detachment of men from Germany was recruited and brought into Britain. They were of the tribe of the Alemanni and their king, Fraomar, came with them as their commander: Hengist's ships were not the first to have crossed the North Sea bringing Germanic warriors into the island, nor was the blood of his men the first to contribute a Germanic element to the variety of Britain's people. Fraomar flourished at about the time of Offa, King of the Angles, and stories of Fraomar's adventure, of the rich province, of the fortunes to be made there and of the green farmland to be won, no doubt reached the warriors of Offa. These tales may well have been passed on to their grandsons and may have provided a further stimulus to the adventure that was to bring them and their whole nation into Britain.

The arrival of Fraomar is certain and well attested. But there is some shadowy evidence that Saxon soldiers and sailors had settled in Britain as early as the AD 270s. For round about that time the northern seas were infested by pirates from the tribes of Germany, Holland and Denmark. Rome stationed a fleet in British waters and manned it with sailors from the selfsame tribes. Later the south-east coast of Britain, from the Wash to the Isle of Wight, was known as the Saxon Shore; almost certainly it was so named after the Saxon and other German sailors who served and settled there.

Even earlier, some time after AD 175, there was yet another influx of people from beyond the borders of the Empire. The Emperor Marcus Aurelius had defeated the Scythians in southern Russia. As tribute after their defeat, Marcus Aurelius demanded that they should furnish five thousand cavalrymen for the Roman army. The men were duly enrolled and were sent to serve in Britain. They, like the other soldiers of the Empire, would have lived out their lives and died there, leaving sons and daughters to grow up as Britons and to add yet a further strand to the tapestry of the island's people.

The nation with whom the Angles and Saxons were to contend and with whom, after decades of bloody struggle they were to merge and mingle, thus contained within itself the blood and character of many nations. The new English people, which was to come into being as a result of this confluence, had roots stretching through all the lands of Europe, reaching indeed across the Hellespont, into the sunlit lands of Asia, to the very shores of the Euphrates. Some may have dreamed of their homelands, of the olive trees and elm-shaded vines of Italy, of the cypress trees of Greece, of the dark pines of Germany, or of the palm trees and cedars of even further lands. But the rich meadows of Cheshire, the valleys of Gloucestershire, and the wooded hills of Lincolnshire became their homes. The wives they took were no doubt frequently Britons, and the children they begot were Britons too. The population became more varied; dark hair and fair hair, blue eyes and brown, began to be seen not only in the barracks but in village and countryside.

III

JUTISH AND SAXON KINGDOMS

B Y the dawn of the fifth century the people of Britain had
not only become cosmopolitan in blood but were linked
through the imperial and religious ties of Rome to Europe
and the world at large. For the greater part of the period of
occupation three legions were stationed in the island and behind
this triple shield Britain prospered; the many peoples became
one people and Christianity flourished. A common citizenship
and a common religion bound together the descendants of Celtic
aboriginals, Italian soldiers, legionaries from afar, and enlisted
tribal troops.

Then, suddenly, the shield was gone. One legion was probably led away by Stilicho to reinforce the continental armies in
the later part of the fourth century. Magnus Maximus, a Spanish
officer who set himself up as Emperor in Britain, removed all the
remaining troops a few years later (in AD 383) to help him on his
ambitious adventure to Rome. The people of Britain were now
alone and had to devise their own defences. As the unity of the
country fell away, there was a revival of the old tribal kingdoms
which had existed when Rome first occupied the land, and
which had been transformed into Romanised states. The kings
of these regions battled against the Picts from Caledonia who
could at last cross at will the great Wall of Hadrian, now bereft
of its garrisons. They battled too against those whom the Roman
chroniclers called Saxons, who may have been Angles or any

52

other of the seafaring German tribes, and who were no longer content to come as pirates but landed troops to fight side by side with the Picts. On at least one occasion, in AD 429, help came to the Britons from the Continent, in the shape of Germanus, the soldier bishop, who led them to triumphant victory.

But by the AD 440s the position had become desperate. The barbarians—both those from beyond the Wall and those from overseas—were ranging the countryside insolently and victoriously. An appeal was sent to Rome, now in the twilight of her imperial day. Rome could send no armies: she, too, was battling for her existence against invading barbarians. Thirty years earlier, in 410, the city had been captured by the Goths—the first time she had fallen to an enemy host for eight hundred triumphant years.

It was now that the summons was sent to Hengist and his men. Vortigern, one of the kings in Britain, apparently remembered Rome's ancient practice of recruiting warlike tribes and settling them in new homes which they would then defend. He knew all too well the ferocity and warlike skills of the tribes in Germany who had so often and so recently come as a scourge to the shores of Britain. It was to those people, therefore, that he turned.

The story of these events was written down many centuries later and the accounts vary. But the basic facts are clear. The Britons sent messages to Germany and invited the men of one of the tribes to enrol in the armies of the island. They would serve under their own chieftains and would be given land, supplies and arms. This was the summons that brought Hengist and his men to the pebble ridge of Pegwell Bay. The year according to tradition was AD 446.

In the countryside where they landed dwelt the tribe of the Cantii. These people had been there when Julius Caesar invaded Kent five hundred years earlier, and now, with the breakdown of Roman rule, they had a king again. But they had become a very different people from their woad-painted ancestors who with chariots and nimble ponies had fought

D

Caesar's men on the beaches and in the woodlands. In Richborough a legion had now been stationed for centuries, and foreign ex-servicemen had no doubt settled in the local farms and villages. Traders and sailors from many lands had come to the Kentish ports and some would have stayed and merged with the Cantii. In this region, the port and fortress of Dover was a key point in the shore defences of Britain. A huge lighthouse, part of which stands gauntly to this day, had been built by the Romans on the cliff top as a guide to the busy channel shipping. The kingdom of the Cantii—the present county of Kent—lay at the heart of the Saxon Shore; if it is true that this shore was named after the Saxon sailors who had settled there, then already some Germanic blood was among the people of the region. Hengist and his men were coming to a land where, along the coast at least, their language had already been heard and their customs seen.

Over all these people the King of the Cantii ruled from his capital of Durovernum—the modern Canterbury. Here the centuries of Roman rule had produced fine buildings, gorgeous with mosaic and splendid with painted rooms. With the decay of Roman power and the decline of Britain's prosperity, an increasing shabbiness now prevailed; but the walls still girded the city and the tall buildings still stood against the sky. The folk still worshipped Christ in the city's churches and the King of the Cantii felt secure in his kingdom. But the strong walls of his capital did not serve to protect him. He was to be dispossessed and his land was destined to become the first of the Anglo-Saxon kingdoms in the island. It is ironical that one of the few British peoples whose name survives should be the Cantii, the first to lose their land to the Germanic invaders.

The King of the Cantii was, as the events make clear, subordinate to King Vortigern. By Vortigern's orders the warriors from the three ships, led by Hengist and his son Aesc (or Oisc), were brought into his kingdom. They went northwards to the Isle of Thanet, were there settled on the good Kentish farmland, and for a time all went well. Hengist's tall, fair men marched with

the armies of Vortigern northwards against the Picts, and found
the warfare to their liking. To them, of course, war was not
only a sport but a source of wealth, and they were everywhere
successful against the Caledonian invaders. They saw on their
campaign the fertility of Britain's cornfields, moving in the
winds like the sea they knew so well, the cattle browsing in the
water meadows, sheep on the round hills, fat acorn-eating pigs
in the weald, oxen at the plough or pulling loaded harvest wains,
game in the forests, and apple groves in the valleys; all these
were promises of a richer homeland than their old country by
the Oder and Rhine rivers, and were seen as possible trophies
of war. For they saw too that the Britons were hard beset,
and that war to them was no joy but a bitter and unwanted
ordeal.

So it was, according to their own account, that within nine
years of their coming they were in revolt against King Vortigern.
At some point, according to later legend, Vortigern found it
politic to grant the whole kingdom of the Cantii, over the head
of the local king, to his mutinous foreign troops. In this way
Hengist, first of the English kings in Britain, ceased to be merely
a commander of a foreign levy and became King of Kent.
According to the *History* of Nennius, a document probably
drawn up some three hundred and fifty years after the events,
and which therefore mingles legend with fact, King Vortigern
married Hengist's daughter and bestowed the kingdom of Kent
upon his father-in-law on that occasion. There is firmer evidence
that Hengist took or received the throne of Kent : for the *Anglo-
Saxon Chronicle* records that in AD 488 his son Oisc succeeded
to the kingdom and was King for twenty-four years. So the first
of the English kingdoms was swiftly founded and swiftly reached
a degree of stability, its second ruler being able to remain in firm
possession for a quarter of a century, until he died.

Nor was there a complete displacement of the old population;
the kingdom of Kent was not by some tidy miracle of history
suddenly and totally inhabited by the new races of Angles and
Saxons, with the original people dying in battle or fleeing as one

man to Wales. That myth is supported neither by probability nor by the scant evidence that remains. First, Hengist's assumption of the kingdom is dated by the *Anglo-Saxon Chronicle* to AD 455. It occurred therefore too swiftly for a kingdom-full of folk, in the small ships then available, to have had time to come over from Germany. For Hengist's men—or, still more unlikely, Hengist's men and the Kentish women—neatly to replace the original inhabitants, there would have had to be enormous numbers of them. Even in Caesar's day, Kent was densely populated and in Roman days probably yet more so; Roman Britain's main ports lay in the kingdom, and ports are populous places. These ports and towns, the large number of Roman villas found in the country, the many Roman roads, all attest the large numbers who dwelt in the kingdom.

True, two years later the *Anglo-Saxon Chronicle* records that 'the Britons left Kent and with great fear fled to London'. But this must refer to the flight of an army, not of a people. Roman London covered about 325 acres—hardly room enough to give refuge to a whole people. In AD 473 the *Chronicle* records a greater flight of the Britons, who 'fled the English like fire'. This was a major breakout by Hengist's men from their original territory, and this time, undoubtedly, not only the army of the Britons but many refugees fled the onset of the English and moved westward. A total depopulation of the kingdom, however, is impossible to conceive.

There is further and more positive evidence that numbers of the old population remained. The English renamed the capital city of their new kingdom Canterbury—originally *Cantwareburg*, the borough (or fortified town) of the people of the Cantii. It is one of the few examples of the survival into modern times of the name of one of the pre-Roman tribes of Britain, and an indication that the English recognised that the original population still dwelt in the city. Moreover the modern name of the county is still the name of the folk of the Celtic kingdom, with the spelling only slightly modified. The name of Walmer recalls that in Saxon times there was a pond still called the Mere of the

Welsh, a suggestion that a large number of the original people remained there.

So the first of the Anglo-Saxon kingdoms was in fact an Anglo-Celtic kingdom and the subjects of Hengist and his successors were an Anglo-Celtic people. Even that nomenclature does not truly convey a picture of the people over whom the descendants of Hengist held sway. Among their subjects were men in whose veins flowed the blood of the legionaries and veterans, of the traders and settlers already described. The swords of Hengist and his son had not merely struck out the boundaries of the first of the English kingdoms. They had carved in miniature a model of the future kingdom of England, where many people of diverse origins, of differing religions and many tongues, became subject to one set of laws, adopted the same customs, spoke the same language, but retained regional differences and regional loyalties. In Kent we can see the first example of the enormous power of ethnic digestion possessed by the Anglo-Saxon people. Kent, with all its mixture of peoples, became a stable English kingdom : the dynasty founded by Hengist and his son Oisc endured for three centuries.

Although Kent is entitled to be called the first of the Anglo-Saxon kingdoms; although the chronicles of the Britons refer to Hengist and his men as Saxons; although Bede refers to the invaders as Angles or Saxons; and although the reference to the island of Oghgul as Hengist's original home has raised the speculation that he and his troops were Angles, they were almost certainly Jutes. The evidence of archaeology is fairly conclusive, and Bede himself states later that the people of Kent were descended from the Jutes. These were the third folk who built the land of England upon the foundations of Roman and Celtic Britain. Precisely where they came from is still in doubt. None of their own traditions or written histories survive. They were closely connected with the Saxons, as is indicated by Tacitus and by later Latin writers. It may be that originally they dwelt in Jutland. But by the time they sailed for Britain they had almost certainly migrated and had become associated with the

Franks of Germany. Certainly, archaeology suggests that the culture of Kent was closely related to the culture of the Franks. We know too that there was a linguistic link. For when the first Christian missionaries came from Rome about a hundred years later, to restore the Christian religion to the now pagan kingdom, it was a group of Franks whom they brought with them to act as interpreters. The tribal affinities of Hengist's men are not precisely known, but the central facts remain. An English kingdom had been established on the soil of Britain a mere twenty or thirty years after the first settlement of the troops from Germany; and it was a kingdom ruled by a Germanic aristocracy of the sword, yet embodying men and women of many different origins.

The name of the Jutish nation is practically forgotten in modern England. For three centuries the Kings of Kent took pride in their descent from Hengist and from Oisc. They were known as the *Oiscingas*, the sons of Oisc, and as races of seamen and adventurers have always done, they loved to count as their ancestor a man who had ventured from afar and founded a new nation—as other men were later to be proud of their descent from the invading Normans or, in a different land, from those who had crossed wider seas in the *Mayflower*. But in AD 762 the last descendants of Hengist died; they were two brothers, King Aethelberht and King Eadberht, who together with the latter's son Eardulf were joint kings in Kent. With them died the old royal house of the first English kingdom, and Kent soon fell under the sway of other powers.

Far more enduring were the names of the later comers, the Saxons and the Angles. The memory of the one survives in the county names of Sussex, Essex and Middlesex—the ancient kingdoms of the South Saxons, the East Saxons and the Middle Saxons; and of the other in the region of East Anglia and in the name of the whole land of England. The blood of their kings has endured no less, for the present royal house of England is descended directly from the first Saxon kings and, through intermarriage, from the first kings of the Angles.

Although it was the Angles who were to give their name

both to the new folk and to the new language, it was the Saxons who first dominated the southern part of the land. It was they who set up the most powerful of the new kingdoms—the kingdom of Wessex, which by the skill of its soldiers and the resolution of its kings was to bring together the diverse and warring peoples of Britain and to form out of them a single nation.

The *Anglo-Saxon Chronicle* reports that in AD 477, only some thirty years after the coming of Hengist and his men, a chieftain named Aelle came to Britain with his three sons, Cymen, Wlencing and Cissa. Aelle, who was the leader of the South Saxons and the founder of their kingdom, came with three ships and landed on the sandy promontory of Selsey Bill, only a few miles south of the great Roman city of Chichester. He marched his men northwards and, very soon after landing, attacked the Britons who had gathered to oppose him. He was victorious, and according to the *Chronicle* many Britons were slain and others fled into the forest of the Weald. The fugitive Britons, once they had made their way over the high ground, would have had the tall barrier of the South Downs between them and the invaders. Remembering the small number of warriors who would have been engaged in this early fighting, it is impossible to conceive that Aelle's men, so soon after landing, could have organised any systematic seeking out and killing of those Britons who took refuge in the thick oak forests. The Saxon band would have been content to dominate the coastline and to occupy the countryside for a few miles inland. Neither the total occupation of the interior nor the extermination of the existing population would have been feasible. Archaeological work bears out the assumption that the pagan Saxons, like their predecessors the Jutes, made no early penetration of the inland areas.

As far as the Jutes are concerned, pagan cemeteries of the first English lie thick in eastern Kent. In the Isle of Thanet where Hengist's men first settled, they are witness to the early occupation of the land by the heathen warriors from Germany. More pagan cemeteries on the mainland of Kent, beyond the

confines of the Isle of Thanet, testify to the breakout of the
early settlers from the lands granted to them by Vortigern, and
to their swift invasion of the kingdom of Kent. But almost all
these cemeteries lie to the east of the Dover-Canterbury road.
The original mixed folk of the Cantii, their independence gone
and now governed by heathen kings, still lived in the forests
and hills of the western part of their old kingdom. In the north
of Kent the evidence points to a similar story. There is a scattering of pagan cemeteries along the coast from Gravesend to
Whitstable, linking up with those in the Isle of Thanet; but
south of the Chatham-Canterbury road there are few.
Christianity did not come to the English kings and people of
Kent until one hundred and fifty years after Hengist's day.

With the Saxons in Sussex, the land of Aelle and his men,
the story is the same. There are clusters of pagan cemeteries
along the coastal strip from Eastbourne to Worthing and none
in the interior to the north. The Sussex Weald, like the Weald
of Kent, was proving a safe refuge to hunted Britons. The tale
told in the *Chronicle* reinforces the evidence of the cemeteries:
in AD 491, a full fifteen years after his arrival, Aelle captured
from the Britons the old Roman fort of Anderida at Pevensey,
which stands at the eastern edge of the coastal strip of pagan
cemeteries and which appears to have marked, at least for a
time, the limit of the advance of the South Saxons.

Place names tell the same story. Just as the royal descendants
of Oisc called themselves the *Oiscingas*, the descendants of other
settlers used similar forms. Hastings was originally a settlement
of people who called themselves *Haestingas* after their first lord
and ancestor. The village of Lancing took its name in a similar
manner, as did all the other place names ending in *ing*. This type
of village name was known to the English while they were still
on the Continent and the form ceased to be used after the sixth
century. Thus names of this kind are a good index to the places
where the new folk had settled within a hundred to a hundred
and fifty years of their first coming; and the evidence of these
names supports that of the cemeteries. For in Sussex they are

mainly to be found along the coastal strip from Pevensey to Selsey. But northwards there are very few, and the forest lands of the Weald were relatively free of early Saxon settlers. Other place names confirm that they went there later, made clearings in the forest and cultivated the land. But there is no evidence of very early settlement or of early depopulation.

Aelle's men, having probably neutralised Chichester in their first attack and having put to flight the army of the Britons based upon that city, appear to have turned eastwards. Their left flank was protected from sudden attack by the Downs and their right by the sea. It was the kind of campaign that was to be often repeated by their descendants in later years and along many different coasts. Though the roads inland were denied to them by strongpoints and defenders, the sea was their pathway and along it the three ships that brought them, reinforced perhaps with craft captured in the havens of the Britons, could advance eastwards with the good west wind filling their sails. From Chichester to Pevensey the numerous towns and villages with *ing* place names speak of the swift conquest and the early settlements along the coast.

The *Chronicle* is silent on the subject of Aelle after his capture of the fort of Pevensey in AD 491. His kingdom by physical occupation appears to have been limited to the narrow tract of land bounded by Chichester to the west, Pevensey to the east, and stretching inland for only a few miles. And yet it is recorded that he was the first to hold the title of *Bretwalda* or Lord of Britain. The *Chronicle* mentions this, almost in passing, in a late entry (AD 827) more than three hundred years after his day. Bede makes the same statement nearly a hundred years earlier and there seems to be no reason to doubt it. Aelle's claim to be Lord of Britain must have been based not on a total conquest of the old Roman province, but on his domination of one or two important centres. The claim was an exaggerated one, based perhaps on ambition rather than achievement. It is none the less significant, for it shows that the invading Saxons saw themselves very early as the successors of the former rulers of the

whole province : and that they conceived the province, from
the earliest days, not merely as a disorganised tract of country
within which they could establish their kingdom, but as a
political whole that should be ruled over by a single power.
They saw themselves as the inheritors of the Roman Island.

Moreover Aelle's ambition shows that the early Saxon kings
did not conceive their kingdoms merely as those regions inhabited by their own Saxon followers. In Aelle's lifetime there had
certainly not been time for a total conquest, a total depopulation
and a total resettlement by a new folk even within his own kingdom of Sussex—still less within the whole province. So Aelle, as
Lord of Britain, saw as his subjects all those who dwelt in the
island, of whatever race.

Celts and Italians, the descendants of the Spanish and Balkan
legionaries, the families of Greek and Egyptian origin, the many
folk in whose veins flowed the blood of Russian cavalrymen,
of Caledonian recruits and of Syrian and Turkish soldiers—all
these could come under the broad sweep of his sword and
sceptre. Whether he could enforce his claim, and whether it was
accepted by all those he sought to govern, are matters of doubt.
But make the claim he did; and, in the individual English kingdoms, as well as in the province as a whole, the separate identity
of the pre-Saxon population was evidently to be lost, except in
Wales, Devon and Cornwall. As Aelle's story also testifies, however, the setting up of Saxon kingdoms and of English kings
did not mean the destruction of the old population. The derelict
Roman villas lay deserted, the last owners having fled to poorer
farmland in safer places, or perhaps having gone as captives
into servitude. But there is no archaeological evidence for widespread sacking, burning and slaughter. Few of the villas that
have been excavated show scars of fire or sword. They tell simply
a tale of desertion and slow decay.

Aelle's claim to be Lord of Britain was not renewed by his
sons and successors, and after his reign the kingdom of the South
Saxons sank into long obscurity. His heirs find no place in the
story and the next Lord of Britain was to come from another

and more powerful kingdom that was established to the west of the South Saxons.

In AD 495, some fifty years after Hengist's men landed in Thanet, the *Anglo-Saxon Chronicle* records the coming of two leaders, Cerdic and his son Cynric, with five ships. Their landing was opposed, for it is said that they fought the Britons on the same day as they came ashore. These two established the kingdom of the West Saxons, and Cerdic became its first king. This great kingdom of Wessex, which was to comprise Somerset, Wiltshire, Berkshire and Hampshire, finally imposed its will over all England, uniting the whole land under one crown. Cerdic became king of the West Saxons in AD 519, and his descendant still reigns in England. He, more than any other single person, may be looked upon as the founder of England and of the English throne.

And yet there is considerable doubt whether Cerdic was himself a Saxon. The *Chronicle* does not refer to the followers who came with him in his five ships as West Saxons. Indeed, a separate entry, under the date of AD 514—nineteen years after Cerdic's arrival in the island—records that the West Saxons then came to Britain with three ships, led by two men named Stuf and Wihtgar. This suggests that Cerdic was not himself a West Saxon, but was later offered their kingdom because of his prowess as a war leader. His name indeed is not Saxon, being almost certainly a form of the modern Welsh Caradoc and strongly suggesting that he was of Celtic stock. If this was so, then his five ships sailed not from Germany but perhaps from Gaul. Maybe he was the descendant of one of the many Britons who had sought refuge across the Channel during the troubled days of the Saxon attacks in the fifth century. His wife may well have been Saxon, for his son Cynric's name is certainly Germanic, and the *Chronicle* later mentions that Stuf and Wihtgar, the West Saxon leaders, were his kinfolk. If all this be true, then besides being the founder of the greatest of the English kingdoms and progenitor of the English kings, Cerdic typifies the new land and the mixed people over whom his seed was to reign for so long. Through him the blood of the Britons as well as of the Saxons was to flow in the veins of the kings of England, and the people of England were to be and are still the subjects of a family that in itself combined the old population and the new.

It was almost certainly during the lifetime of Cerdic that the Britons stoutly renewed their resistance to the invaders, led by Arthur their great war leader. According to the British story, Arthur united the divided British kings and fought twelve battles against the English. In the last, the battle of Mount Badon, he routed the English, and the Britons enjoyed a long respite from attack. For them the golden age had returned, something of Roman order and old prosperity was restored.

The Battle of Mount Badon was probably fought in AD 517 and the West Saxons' offer of their kingdom to Cerdic in AD 519 may have been a result of the disarray in which they then found themselves; their armies in desperate need of reorganisation and refitting, they needed a powerful and resolute leader.

Cerdic, now king of the infant kingdom of Wessex, resumed the war, fighting the Britons in the year he took the throne and again eight years later. But there was no swift advance inland. In AD 530 he took the Isle of Wight, which he gave to his two kinfolk Stuf and Wihtgar, and four years later he died. The kingdom which he bequeathed to his son Cynric was both strong and stable. Eighteen years later, Cynric was fighting far to the west and captured the stronghold of Old Sarum in Wiltshire. Twenty-five years later, the descendants of Cerdic had fought their way into Gloucester, Cirencester and Bath; the whole of south-west England was theirs and Wessex had become a major power.

Ceawlin, successor to Cynric, fought not only against the Britons, but imposed his will upon the kingdom of Kent. He, like Aelle but with greater justification, took the title of *Bretwalda*, Lord of Britain. Once more we have the concept of a united country, with the authority of one king reigning over the lesser kingdoms and holding sway over all the people of the former Roman province. Successful though Wessex undoubtedly was, and victorious in her wars, Ceawlin's title was not based upon a complete occupation of the whole country, still less upon a total resettlement of the whole land by Saxons. The West Saxons had marched far and had defeated many enemies, both Saxon and Celtic, but the very length of time they took for their conquest argues against any dramatic and wholesale destruction of the local people. Ceawlin marched triumphantly into the city of Bath in AD 577, more than eighty years after Cerdic, his great forbear, had brought his five ships to Britain. For the Saxon armies to have taken eighty years to march into the west country permits no conception of irresolute and unwarlike Britons fleeing in despair to the Welsh hills. Many of them, as we shall see, stayed on in lands dominated by the West Saxons and Ceawlin, Lord of Britain, claimed all as his subjects.

The place names suggest that Wessex, unlike Sussex, had been invaded not so much by sea from the south coast as by the waterway of the Thames. There are no *ing* names along the coastal strip west of Portsmouth, and no pagan cemeteries, to tell of any early settlement from the sea. But along the Thames Valley there are names of this kind and cemeteries too. In Wiltshire and Hampshire, although these were part of the kingdom of Wessex, pagan Saxon burials are comparatively rare. This again indicates that in the heart of the kingdom there had been no early planting of Saxon people, though the power of the Saxon kings had penetrated and triumphed.

The kingdom of Wessex appears to have included a region occupied not by Saxons but by Jutes. Bede records that the people of Kent (the *Cantuarii*) and the people of the Isle of Wight (the *Victuarii*) were descended from the Jutes. He adds that the people on the mainland of Wessex opposite the Isle of Wight were of the same descent, and were still known as the Jutish nation in his day. Some memory of this survived in local place names for over a thousand years. Florence of Worcester, writing of the death of William II, speaks of the New Forest 'which in English is called *Ytene*'; this word ('of the Jutes') supports Bede's statement. So too does archaeology, for the graves of this area and of the Isle of Wight, together with the offerings laid in them, show a striking resemblance to those of Kent.

From Wessex in the seventh century comes dramatic evidence for the survival of the Celts within the new kingdom. Between AD 685 and AD 688 Wessex was on the march. Kent was conquered, a king of Sussex slain, and the Isle of Wight invaded and captured. The story of these wars is not particularly remarkable. They were part of the long struggle between the many English kingdoms, in which the weaker vanished and the stronger increased their power. The two years' campaign upon which Wessex then embarked can be paralleled in other struggles and in other wars of the period. But what is remarkable is the name of the king under whom they marched—Ceadwalla; for this is British and not Saxon. How did the West Saxons at this date, over two hundred years after they had seized and settled their kingdom, have as their leader a man with a British name?

Some nine years earlier (in AD 676) a prince named Centwine had succeeded to the throne of Wessex. He was a great-great-grandson of the now legendary Cerdic, first king of the West Saxons in the days of the invasion some two hundred years earlier. Those ancient days were now lost in the mist of legend, but Centwine's title to the kingdom was based upon direct descent from his great ancestor, and was undoubted. He continued the stern task of his predecessors and, in the sixth year of his reign, he conducted a victorious campaign against the Britons; the *Anglo-Saxon Chronicle* tells us that he drove them as far as the sea.

Ceadwalla was his kinsman, and like him a direct descendant of the great Cerdic. The latter's son Cynric had left two sons: King Centwine was a grandson of one of these, and Ceadwalla a great-great-grandson of the other. He was only a youth when Centwine became king. There had been no kings in Ceadwalla's branch of the family. Centwine, whose ancestors had been kings before him, seemed in an unchallengeable position and his grip on the sceptre of Wessex appeared secure.

Ceadwalla had as a boy been exiled from his native land. Perhaps he was already known to be ambitious and Centwine, though firmly established as king, held it safer not to allow Ceadwalla to live too close to a throne which his pride coveted and to which his birth gave him some right to aspire. But he was not idle in exile, nor was his ambition diminished by distance from his own land. The description given by Tacitus of the tribes of Germany six hundred years earlier is recalled, for the tradition that the leader would reward his followers by the plunder they won in battle still persisted: as Cerdic had won a kingdom by war, and as countless other Saxon leaders had similarly gained riches, so the young prince went out to seek his fortune, with a group of companions. They marched into Sussex, plundering and laying waste. The king of the South Saxons, Aethelwalh, was killed in the fighting, but any hopes that Ceadwalla might have entertained of seizing the kingdom of Sussex were frustrated. He and his men were defeated by two leaders of the South Saxons and driven back over the frontier.

He had now, in his late twenties, had his first taste of adventure and had almost won a kingdom. In AD 685 the *Anglo-Saxon Chronicle* records that he began to contend for the kingdom of Wessex, assisted by his brother Mul. His attempt was successful and by the following year he was securely seated upon the throne, having ousted his kinsman King Centwine. However, his ambition was not satisfied and he at once began an attempt to bring the neighbouring territories under his rule. In AD 686 he and his brother Mul attacked the kingdom of Kent and laid it waste. He turned westwards into the land held by the Jutes and invaded the Isle of Wight. The two young princes of the island fled to the mainland where they were pursued and killed. Ceadwalla himself was severely wounded in the fighting, but he nevertheless continued his campaigns; Sussex fell to him, and one of the two leaders who had defeated him on the occasion of his earlier invasion was killed. Ceadwalla had taken his revenge.

In addition to his recorded campaigns, he appears to have had authority in Surrey: a charter of his makes a gift to the church of land around Farnham. So he was now the master of almost all southern England, of Wessex, Sussex, Surrey and Kent. He had pointed the way to the West Saxons and had demonstrated the possibility of the wide conquests they were later to make. But, within twelve months of his triumph, there came tragic news. His brother Mul, together with twelve of his men, had been burned alive by the men of Kent; according to William of Malmesbury, the house in which they had taken refuge was set alight. This horrible and inhuman act was long remembered in Wessex; the *Chronicle* mentions it twice as if it were the most important event in Ceadwalla's brief reign. He assembled his army, marched into Kent and again laid that kingdom waste.

During all this while, although not a baptised Christian, Ceadwalla had been a friend to the church. The religion was still new in the English kingdoms; with the Britons it was deeper-rooted, having been established among them in Roman days. Some time in the summer of AD 688, when he was at the height of his power, a mere three years after becoming King of Wessex, and when his rule ran over many kingdoms, Ceadwalla stepped down from the throne, renounced his crown, and set out on the long journey to Rome. He had a great desire to be baptised by the Pope himself and to be formally admitted into the church within the walls of St Peter's; and during his journey, at a town near Calais he made a gift of money to a church. He was received by Pope Sergius, and Bede records that he was baptised during the Easter festival of AD 689, some eight or nine months after setting sail from Wessex. The Pope gave him the Christian name of Peter, and Ceadwalla was invested with the white robes which were at that time worn by the newly baptised for the space of a week.

But before he laid his baptismal robes aside, King Ceadwalla fell ill. Perhaps it was the result of the old wound he had taken on the Isle of Wight, though the nature of his malady is not recorded. Whatever it was, he could not be cured and, according to Bede, he died on the thirtieth of April. The Pope caused his tomb to be erected in St Peter's church and over it was carved an inscription recounting in verse how King Ceadwalla had renounced his riches, his kingdom, his great treasures and his hopes of fame, for the love of God. Beneath the verses a prose inscription recorded that he was about thirty when he died, and gave the date of the burial of 'Ceadwalla, also known as Peter, King of the Saxons'.

King of the Saxons he most certainly was, and of the royal line of Wessex. Yet his name as we have noted was British. Since Cerdic, founder of the line, all the recorded names of the kings and princes of Wessex had been Saxon. Names were not given lightly in those days, and it is highly unlikely that Coenberht his father had, by a mere whim, selected a British name for him. It is also unlikely that Coenberht had any thought of the British origins of the royal house in Cerdic, two hundred years before. The only reasonable explanation is that Coenberht had married a Briton and that she had had a voice in choosing a name for their son.

When, in Chapter V, we look at the laws of Wessex drawn up by Ceadwalla's successor, it will be shown that there were many Britons dwelling peacefully in the kingdom of the West Saxons. If Coenberht had found his bride from among them, then she is evidence that there were aristocratic families of Britons with whom a prince of Wessex was not ashamed to be allied; not merely poor peasants or slaves had stayed on in the Saxon kingdoms. If, on the other hand, Coenberht had married a princess from one of the kingdoms of the Britons, then there must have been contact between the two peoples in matters other than war, and periods of peace must have separated the periods of hostility. Penda's story has told as much already, and has shown how another Saxon king could find friends and allies among the kings of the Britons. In either case, Coenberht's marriage to a Briton would not have been unique. What happened to a prince would often have happened to more lowly folk. Ceadwalla, King of the Saxons, would certainly not have been the only Englishman in whose veins flowed the blood of the Britons. He is a symbol of the many forgotten contacts that

E

took place between the new and the old inhabitants of the island.

There is much in his brief and violent history that could be explained by his mixed ancestry. His early exile might have been due not merely to his ambition. Perhaps the King of Wessex had disapproved of his kinsman's marriage to a Briton, and perhaps Ceadwalla's banishment had been a mark of that displeasure. His special devotion to Christianity may have owed something to his mother, whose family, unlike the family of her husband, might have been Christians for centuries. It is to be noted too that throughout his brief and tumultuous reign Ceadwalla's sword was wielded against the other English kingdoms. There is no record of his having, like his predecessor, made any thrust against the Britons. He was seeking the unification of all the Saxon kingdoms of the south, rather than the conquest of new land from the Britons. His aim was to be king of all the Saxon peoples south of the Thames and Severn and to rival the greatness of the Angle kingdoms of the north. This and more his successors in Wessex were to achieve.

The Saxons set up two other kingdoms, neither of which could compare in military glory or ultimate political success with the land of Wessex. These were the lands of the East Saxons and of the Middle Saxons. The former left its name to the modern county of Essex but it comprised part of Hertfordshire as well. In Essex itself pagan Saxon remains are few. Most of them lie along the Thames Estuary, and the burials are similar to those of Kent. They may be evidence of travellers and emigrants from the latter kingdom rather than of new settlers from the Continent. On the other hand there is a good scattering of early Saxon place names, both of the *ing* type and those containing the names of Saxon gods. There was thus some early occupation, though no great numbers. Roman Essex was itself but sparsely inhabited; there are no villas in the southern section of the county. Apart from the important city of Colchester, whose massive walls stand to this day, and the great fort at Bradwell, Roman remains are few. They indicate a scattered population, for the most part sunk in poverty. The Saxons would have met with little resistance; their own sparse population, as indicated by the scarcity of archaeological evidence, would have had no need to dispossess the local Britons. Many Celtic place names still survive in Essex, strongly supporting this theory. In the western part of the kingdom, in what is now Hertfordshire, early Saxon settlements are rarer and British survival perhaps more extensive.

None of the Kings of Essex achieved greatness or is strongly remembered in the story of the Anglo-Saxon people. Yet they had two marks of distinction. First, all the other royal houses in the new kingdoms claimed their descent from the god Woden. (Later, when Christianity came to them, they pushed the genealogy still further back, to Adam!) The kings of Essex traced their line from Seaxneat, the special god of the Saxons, a god still worshipped by the Saxons on the Continent some three hundred years after the coming of the new people into Britain. Next, the great city of London lay within their kingdom. Its Roman walls still standing as a formidable defence, its docks and wharves still perhaps serviceable, it would have been a powerful asset—both military and commercial—in the hands of a resolute and ambitious dynasty. But the East Saxons made nothing of its potential strength. It is not certain, indeed, that London ever fell to the first Saxon arrivals. Its stout walls might easily have been defended by its inhabitants, and its storehouses could have helped them to withstand a long siege; and the city may in fact have been counted as barely worth a battle by the land-hungry invaders, who were more intent upon finding good farmland than upon occupying buildings and paved streets. *Londinium* alone among the cities of Britain, retained its Roman name unchanged through the centuries, save for the omission of its latinised ending. To most of the names of the dead Roman cities the Saxons added the word *ceaster*, being their version of the Latin *castra*, a camp; *Venta* became Winchester, *Glaevum* became Gloucester and *Corinium* became Cirencester. Two other cities approach, but do not equal, London's continuity of name. *Lindum Colonia* retains a name close to the original—Lincoln;

and here, where Bede mentions that the English appointed a
prefect of the city, a phrase suggesting that city life of a kind
had long continued, there are virtually no pagan Saxon cemeteries. York, too, echoes its old name, *Eboracum*, and as described
in the next chapter, it is known that it was long held by the
Britons. So, though lacking such direct evidence, there is reason
to believe that London also held out, and for a while survived
as an island in the rising tide of Saxon occupation.

There are at least grounds for speculation. Do Ludgate Hill
and Billingsgate still enshrine the names of the British kings, Lud
and Bellinus, commemorated with no interruption since Celtic
times? Does the penny struck by King Alfred in the London
mint, and bearing London's name in interlocked letters of
strangely Roman design, indicate the survival of old techniques
in the mint originally set up by the Romans in the city? And is
the ancient custom whereby Kings and Queens of England are
met by London's chief magistrate at the gate before entering the
city a relic of some ancient and forgotten treaty under which the
independent inhabitants of London maintained a special
relationship with the English kings? What were the special rights
of the Londoners which William the Conqueror ratified in his
Charter, and which even then were described as being immemorial? Why, when Augustine appointed bishops among the
English, did the Pope (as Bede tells us) enjoin him to arrange
that the Bishop of London, unlike the others, should be consecrated by his own synod? Did this mean that Roman Christianity had survived in the city even through Saxon times, in a
semi-independent Romano-Celtic society?

Certainly, if a town of the size and importance of London had
fallen to the Saxons, the event could be expected to have found
a triumphant place in the *Anglo-Saxon Chronicle*. But the record
is silent. Within, yet not a part of, the new kingdom of the East
Saxons, London's cosmopolitan population, the descendants of
the first Celtic inhabitants and of the foreign traders and merchants, may well have dwelt on in the shabby buildings,
maintaining some of the city's old customs, keeping alive through

years of squalor and ignorance the memory of old kings and ancient gods.

In the county name of Middlesex lies enshrined the memory of the kingdom of the Middle Saxons. Like their neighbours the East Saxons, they never matched the power of the men of Wessex, yet it may be inferred that in their day they were powerful and held wide sway. For Surrey, lying to the south across the

SAXON PLOUGH

river Thames, was once *Suth-rige*, the southern region, dependent upon and indeed part of the kingdom of the Middle Saxons to the north. In Middlesex early Saxon place names are even scantier than in Essex. The scattering of pagan cemeteries lie mainly in the north of the kingdom, in the open country that sweeps north-eastwards from the upper Thames. The *Anglo-Saxon Chronicle* tells nothing about the conquest of this region by the Middle Saxons, nor are the names of their kings recorded. Yet early settlement certainly took place. Harrow for example was an important centre of heathen worship and therefore points to a large Saxon population existing there in the sixth century and maybe before.

There is a hint in Nennius's *History of the Britons*, a book based on Celtic sources, that the kingdom of Middlesex was ceded to the invaders by Vortigern in a treaty which included Essex and Sussex. If this tradition contains some grain of truth it would explain many things: the evidence in Sussex which has already been noted of the early Saxon conquest being limited to the coastal belt; the scant Saxon settlements in Essex; and the very sparse evidence of any early Saxon occupation of Middlesex. If these kingdoms were in fact conveyed to the Saxons by negotiation and treaty, then the picture given by place names and archaeology is logical and acceptable. Already possessed of political power under the treaty, the Saxons had no need to wage continued war. They settled where they wished, taking as much land as they needed, leaving considerable areas untouched and the original population relatively undisturbed. The Celtic folk—the Trinovantes of Essex, the Catuvellauni of Middlesex, and the Regni of Sussex—are likely to have continued to dwell in the new kingdom. Subject to foreign kings, with their lands at the mercy of the new settlers and their deserted cities falling into slow ruin, they may have in part survived and added their blood to the blood of England.

IV

THE KINGDOMS OF THE ANGLES

I N the days of the Roman occupation, the tribe of the Brigantes lived to the north of the river Humber. They had in their day been a great military power and they had early thrown in their lot with the Romans; when Caractacus, the British hero who waged persistent and resolute war against the armies of Claudius, sought refuge with Cartimandua, Queen of the Brigantes, she handed him over as a captive to his pursuers. No doubt she and her subjects enjoyed the favour and protection of the authorities and continued to dwell in their old land under the Roman power.

However, thirty years after the invasion, war broke out between the Roman government and the Brigantes. The Ninth Legion marched against them and set up its base camp in the North. Upon the site was later built the great military centre of *Eboracum*, girt with strong walls and later protected by a great multiangular tower whose ruins stand to this day. York grew to be the most northerly, and one of the most important, of the military centres of the whole Roman Empire. It was a base for many campaigns against the tribes of Caledonia and became the headquarters of the senior military commander in Britain. It was visited by emperors and at one period contained an official imperial residence. Moreover, as already seen, it became a *colonia*—a settlement of ex-servicemen who were given grants of land round about. Mingled with the

Celtic blood of the Brigantes was now the blood of foreign legionaries who cultivated their fields on the hill slopes and in the fertile valleys, raised their families and merged gradually with the older folk.

The Romans had not neglected the seaward defences of the region. Some fifty years before the coming of the Saxons there is archaeological evidence for the manning by the Roman forces of a series of forts and signal stations built on high points along the Yorkshire coast. Hostile ships were crossing the North Sea from Germany and the fair-haired sailors were already coming ashore as pirates and raiders—though not yet as settlers. The vigilance of Britain's watchmen was to reinforce the valour of her soldiers, who could now be deployed in good time to oppose any landing.

Into this area, well fortified, enriched by a long and proud military tradition and knitted together by a network of good roads that could give speedy mobility to its defenders, the Angles came and there built great kingdoms. The coming of Hengist's men to the Kentish coast has been the theme of legend and is widely remembered. The landing of Cerdic, ancestor of the kings of Wessex and of all England, has been commemorated by the scribes of Wessex. But the coming of the Angles to the hills of Yorkshire and the setting up of their kingdoms in the north country, though as stirring a tale as anything that the south can offer, remains unrecorded.

North of the river Humber there grew the kingdoms of Northumbria. One manuscript copy of Bede's book contains a list of the kings of that region which records that Ida was the first English king to rule there; his reign began in AD 547, just a hundred years after the coming of Hengist, and lasted for twelve years. Substantially the same list is given by Nennius, drawn from Celtic sources. Nennius gives the name of Ida's father as Eobba, indicating that the Angles did not set up a formal kingdom when they first landed, since Eobba himself was not a king. Moreover, telling the story from the Celtic point of view, he does not credit Ida with a kingdom, but reports merely that he held regions in northern Britain, beyond the river Humber. Nennius too states that Ida governed for twelve years.

According to the Bede manuscript, the seventh of the Kings of Northumbria was Hussa and, from the years ascribed to the reign of his predecessor, he must have come to the throne in AD 585 and died in AD 592. Nennius says that this king, Hussa, fought against four Kings of the Britons—Urbgen, Rydderch, Guallauc and Morcant. So thirty-eight years after the foundation of Northumbria there were still Celtic kingdoms in the north which could still wage successful war. Nennius records that Urbgen (who is no doubt the King Urien of the Arthurian romances) had fought against Theodric, Hussa's predecessor, whose reign had ended some six years earlier. Thus Urbgen maintained his kingdom and his armies for six years and more; and the Celtic warriors (among whom were no doubt numbered the descendants of foreign legionaries from the countryside around York) were fighting stubbornly and on equal terms with the warlike English. Nor were their battles always defensive. On one occasion Urbgen forced his English adversaries to take refuge in the 'island of Metcaut' and beset them there for three days and nights.

The Celts of the north appear in fact to have formed an alliance against the intruding English. The fact that four of their kings together fought against King Hussa of Northumbria is an indication of this. Moreover, Rydderch, the second of the Celtic kings mentioned by Nennius, came from Dumbarton and was King of Strathclyde. Warned, perhaps, by the fate of the Britons in the south, the Celtic kings of the north realised and combined against the common danger. Yet of one sterner warning they remained heedless. The resistance of the Britons in the south had finally collapsed in jealous quarrels and civil war. Forgetful until too late of the remorseless threat of the Saxons, the Celtic kings of the south had fought among themselves in a struggle for power and authority; with the result that both power and authority passed finally to the more united Saxons. The pages of Gildas, the monk who recorded the fruitless struggle of his fellow Britons, are full of the bitterness of that disunity and of its final outcome. Tragically, something of this was repeated in the lands north of the Humber. For after his endurance and successes against the English, the great Urbgen was murdered at the instigation of Morcant, his one-time ally. Morcant's treachery was due to envy because Urbgen was the mightiest of all kings in waging war; he left a name and reputation that lived on in legend.

However, the resistance of the Britons did not die with him. Some thirty years later, in AD 617, King Edwin succeeded to the throne of Northumbria which, under his predecessor Aethilfrid, had become a great and dominant English kingdom. There were many plots against his life; the King of Wessex conspired against him as did Aethilfrid. He escaped these perils and reigned triumphantly for many years. He was married to the daughter of the King of Kent and had become a Christian, but neither his victorious reputation nor the religion which he now shared with the Christian Britons was proof against the latters' persistent and unbending hostility. One of the British leaders of the north, King Cadwallon, allied himself with the English kingdom of Mercia and brought Edwin to battle on the plains near Doncaster. There King Edwin died, in AD 633, as did his son Osfrid, while his other son Eadfrid fled into Mercia and was killed there. The greatness of Northumbria lay in ruins.

The chronicles of the Britons record their triumph. Nennius tells of the death of Edwin and of his two sons at the hands of *Catguollauni regis Guendotae regionis*, of Cadwallon, King of the kingdom of Gwynedd. Bede also tells the story and adds an important detail: after the battle King Edwin's head was struck off and taken to York. Edwin's cousin Osric then succeeded to the throne of Deira, one of the provinces into which Northumbria had been split, after its defeat, while the other province, Bernicia, was given to another prince. Bede reports that Osric sought to avenge the dead Edwin and marched against Cadwallon; and in this context Bede states specifically that

Cadwallon held York as his capital city. This is immensely important. It shows that one of the greatest of the Roman cities and military centres in Britain was still in the hands of the Britons, and was the capital of a British kingdom, nearly two hundred years after the first coming of the English and almost a hundred years after the setting up of the English kingdom of Northumbria. The Britons were putting to good purpose the stout defences and strong walls which their ancestors had raised.

And Cadwallon the Briton held on successfully against the siege and assaults of Osric's English. Finally he led his men in a fierce sally from the city gates and fell upon his enemies. King Osric was killed in the merciless and bitter fighting; and Cadwallon had claimed a second English king as a victim of his prowess. In the following year he claimed his third, slaying Eanfrith the King of Bernicia, and took possession of the whole of Northumbria. The cause of the Britons was victorious throughout the north. That Cadwallon could for so long maintain an army in the field at such a late date is clear evidence of the tenacity of the Britons and of their long survival as an organised nation. There can be little doubt that modern Englishmen from the counties north of the Humber are the descendants not merely of the Angles of Northumbria, but of the original Celtic population and of the ex-servicemen from beyond the seas whose progeny had followed the standard of Cadwallon as valorously as ever their ancestors had followed the eagles of Rome.

Oswald, brother of the dead King Eanfrith of Bernicia, finally recovered the kingdom for the English and Cadwallon died in the fighting. The English called the action the Battle of *Deniseburn* (probably AD 634), which is Rowley Water in Northumberland. The Britons named it the Battle of *Catscaul* or *Cantscaul*—the Battle within the Wall, and in their chronicles they recorded the death of Cadwallon, one of their greatest heroes. After his victory Oswald, like Edwin before him, took the title of *Bretwalda*, Lord of Britain, and was the sixth English king to do so.

Meantime other Angles had settled in other lands south of the

ANGLO·SAXON
ENGLAND

Strathclyde

KINGDOM OF NORTHUMBRIA

Bernicia

Hadrians Wall

Deira

NORTH

SEA

Isle of Man

York

IRISH SEA

Elmet

Lindsey

Chester

Lincoln

The
Wash

Gwynedd

Nottingham

Derby

WALES

Leicester

Stamford

East
Angles

Ely

KINGDOM OF MERCIA

Dyfed

Hwicce

KINGDOM
OF THE
MIDDLE
SAXONS

KINGDOM OF
THE EAST
SAXONS

Bath

London

Thames
Estuary

Bristol Channel

KINGDOM OF THE WEST SAXONS

Winchester

KINGDOM
OF KENT

Canterbury

Salisbury

KINGDOM OF THE
SOUTH SAXONS

Hastings

CORNWALL (West Wales)

Portland

Isle of Wight

Humber and had set up the Kingdom of Mercia. Because they had for long been thrusting against the British kingdoms lying to their west, the Angles of this region called themselves the *Mierce*, the folk of the Marches, or the border people. This name the kingdom retained long after it had ceased to be a mere frontier province and had grown extensive and powerful. Mercia's beginnings lie in settlements along the valley of the Trent, with the earliest English inhabitants moving southwards from Northumbria rather than coming in new seaborne invasions from Germany. Pagan cemeteries follow the line of the river southwards. Several place names in the Midlands suggest that the first settlements took place in heathen times, before the end of the sixth century when Augustine brought Christianity to the English. Wednesbury and Wednesfield were once the burgh (or fortified place) and the field or open country of the god Woden, from whom the Kings of Mercia were to claim their descent. Other intruders may have come westwards and southwards as emigrants from the Angle kingdom of Lindsey, which lay between the Humber and the Wash and which was centred on the Roman city of Lincoln. To the north-west of Mercia stood the British kingdom of Elmet which maintained its independence into the late AD 600s when it was conquered by King Edwin of Northumbria. Memory of Elmet, kingdom of the Britons, long survived and the name remains as part of village names in the West Riding of Yorkshire to this day.

Throughout the Midland counties the evidence suggests a slow and irregular advance of the English, with final political dominance coming much later than in the south. Again the process was too slow for any sudden sweeping away of the old population. The lack of any tradition of the early days of Mercia supports this view. There seem to have been no great victories to be commemorated and no early heroes whose battles against the Britons were remembered. In fact the first Mercian king to achieve fame as a military leader was Penda, who flourished between AD 620 and AD 654. His victories were against the Saxons of Wessex and against his kin in Northumbria and in other Anglian kingdoms. Indeed the Britons were not his enemies but his allies, for he joined forces and fought side by side with their king, Cadwallon. Mercia, in the person of Penda, evidently accepted the continued existence of Cadwallon's British kingdom as a permanent fact. Penda, still a heathen, fought with the Christian Cadwallon against the Christian Edwin, and later against the Christian rulers of other English kingdoms. His wars were not motivated by religion or race; they had as their sole aim the glory of Mercia and the extension of her power.

KING OFFA (757-96 AD), FROM A COIN

Of all the English kings now established in the island, Penda was the most aristocratic, being royally descended. Hengist had won the kingdom of Kent by blood and by swordplay. Cerdic had been given the sceptre of Wessex because of his prowess and leadership. The heirs of these two men, and of the other English kings, knew that their families had become royal only since arrival in the island. Ancient wars had given them regality and new wars might strip them of their honour. But Penda the Angle came from his people's old royal house; he was the direct lineal descendant of that King Offa who had ruled the Angles in Germany before they came to Britain and who had fought a duel by the banks of the Eider. Sometime between AD 811 and 814, the pedigree of the Kings of Mercia was written down, and two ninth-century copies of it survive—one in the British Museum and one at Corpus Christi College, Cambridge. Penda appears as being the eighth generation from Offa, while the latter is shown as descended through five generations from the god Woden. The chronology of events suggests that it was Offa's great-grandson, Icel, who first came to Britain; and he came, of course, not as a mere fighting adventurer like Hengist and Cerdic, but as a descendant of kings and as a king in his own right.

Penda was ambitious, and not only achieved the expansion of his own kingdom of Mercia, but set his son Peada upon the throne of the Middle Anglians. Perhaps he was fired by the thought that the house of Offa might come to rule over the whole province of Britain. In spite of his aggressive and successful policy this was not to be : it was the kings of Wessex, descendants of Cerdic, who were to unite the whole land and whose heirs were to sit upon the throne of England. Yet, in part, Penda's dream was to be fulfilled. For a princess of his family was later to marry Alfred of Wessex, of the house of Cerdic, and through this union the two royal lines came together. The seed of Offa and the seed of Cerdic are joined in the present royal house of England.

Penda's first adventure symbolised and foreshadowed this union. The *Anglo-Saxon Chronicle* records that four years before he became king, he was fighting against the West Saxons at Cirencester (AD 628), and that an agreement was reached there between him and Wessex. This can only mean that Cirencester and the Saxon lands round about were yielded to Penda. Under him therefore Saxons and Angles for the first time, though in a limited area, became subjects of one lord. It was thus round the old Roman city of *Corinium* and along the valley of the Severn that the first truly Anglo-Saxon people was established, the region becoming known as the kingdom of the *Hwicce*. These people (whose name is still commemorated in Wychwood Forest) dwelt in Worcestershire, Gloucestershire and Warwickshire. Cirencester had not fallen to the West Saxons until AD 577, eighty years after Cerdic's landing; the Britons had not been swiftly ousted from their lands so far to the west, and among the *Hwicce* there must have dwelt many of the old stock. For a hundred and fifty years the *Hwicce* had their own kings, who were dependent upon the kings of Mercia but who nevertheless maintained the separate existence of their region.

In the north as we have seen, the British King Cadwallon had attacked the English kingdom of Northumbria. Penda joined forces with him and Northumbria, its power destroyed, was broken into the two kingdoms of Bernicia and Deira. For a brief while Penda was supreme. Finally, in order to complete his enemies' overthrow, he marched against Deira with a huge army. Among his allies were many British kings, and again the Britons appear as still numerous, still well-organised, and still able to place large armies in the field. In the ensuing battle Penda died (AD 654), together with his British allies. Northumbria's power was re-established and for a while Mercia became a mere province of her northern neighbour.

But Penda had left a son, Wulfhere, who had gone into hiding after the defeat of his father, and who emerged to proclaim himself King of Mercia. Again the Angles had a descendant of Offa at their head, and again they marched to victory. Wulfhere's power extended as far south as the Thames, and the Kings of Essex acknowledged him as their overlord. He was able to gather together an army drawn from many regions of southern England and to make a determined but unsuccessful challenge to the power of Northumbria. Although his host was defeated, he had briefly shown that Angles and Saxons could unite and that wars between the English kingdoms in Britain were not nationalistic, but were struggles between rival political forces. His father Penda before him, by allying himself with Cadwallon the Briton, had taught a similar lesson. Mercia and her kings had demonstrated that the lands of the old Roman province were potentially a single entity, and that a single nation could be built out of the many people now inhabiting the island. But it was left not to their descendants the Angles, but to the Saxons of Wessex to create that unity and to build the one nation.

Page 85: (above) St Mark, from the *Lindisfarne Gospels*, an Anglo-Saxon manuscript of about AD 700; (right) a page from the *Anglo-Saxon Chronicle* for the year AD 871, recording the victory of King Aethelred and his brother Alfred over the Danes at Ashdown.

Page 86: (*above*) Alfred's jewel, of gold and enamel with a portrait of a man holding two sceptres or wands. It was found on the Isle of Aethelney in Somerset; (*below*) side view of the jewel showing the first two words of the inscription: AELFRED ME HET GEWYRCAN—Alfred had me made.

V

THE RULE OF LAW

LONG before the Angles, Saxons and Jutes had come to Britain their kings had ruled them in a manner that was limited by ancient custom. We read in the pages of Tacitus that the kings of the tribes of Germany possessed no arbitrary or unlimited power. The limitations set upon their rights were probably never reduced to writing. Custom and precedent, together with an impatient and swift resentment against tyranny, would have been the most important checks upon a chief's behaviour. Among the Anglo-Saxon people of the modern world these factors are still present and are still almost as effective and powerful as written rules.

In their original lands the tribes had been insulated from the Roman practice of codified and formal laws. Their contacts with Rome had been only those of war and trade. Their dense forests, the wide Rhine river, the remoteness of their tribal centres, and their jealous independence from foreign rule, had all served to keep their society conservative and their customs unmodified.

In Britain the case was otherwise. They found themselves in a land which for four hundred years had been subject to Rome and to all the influences of Roman practice. True, Rome's military power had departed before they came, but the Roman towns were still standing and Roman methods of government lingered in at least some of the cities, albeit in shadowy form, distorted by time and by ignorance. As already seen, the first English came into close contact with some of the British kingdoms; the northern British kingdom of Elmet was not absorbed by Northumbria until the seventh century. Penda of Mercia numbered Cadwallon and many other British kings among his associates. Through contacts of this kind the early English kings saw something of the more formal methods of Roman and quasi-Roman governments. They would have found moreover that in many of these British kingdoms learning and the art of writing were highly esteemed. A hundred years after the coming of Hengist's men into Kent, the Britons found a learned and devoted chronicler in the person of Gildas the monk : eloquent, erudite, devoted to the British cause and to the Christian religion which the Romans had introduced, Gildas was a writer of distinction. The chronicle of Nennius shows that other Britons were keeping written records of their wars.

Finally, though in Germany the tribes had had no contact with the Christian religion, they came under its direct influence in the island of Britain. Kent, first of the English kingdoms to be founded, was the first to be converted. In AD 597 St Augustine came from Rome to the Isle of Thanet and preached to the subjects of King Aethelberht. Now, for the first time, an English king met a representative of the Christian Church of Rome, a body which by now was highly organised, sophisticated and literate. Within a very few years of his conversion, King Aethelberht caused the laws of his kingdom to be written down; with him, tribal custom and ancient practice began to give way to a formal legal system. The surrender was never complete, however; custom, practice and precedent continued and indeed continue to count for much with the English people.

Bede, writing a century or so after the laws of Aethelberht had been recorded, seems to have been very conscious of the break with the past which they represented. For in recording the death of King Aethelberht he mentions the King's laws and adds that they were drawn up 'in the Roman manner'. The laws in fact had little or nothing in common with Roman law; it was the fact that they were reduced to writing in an orderly fashion that caused the comparison.

The general tenor of Aethelberht's laws reminds us forcibly of the tribal laws as described by Tacitus. For, as in his day, guilt was expiated by a series of fines or monetary compensation. The seventh-century ruler of Kent followed closely the practices of his first-century ancestors in Germany. Tacitus had noted that among the German tribes certain offences were punished by fines of fixed numbers of horses or cattle; half of these fines went to the king and half to the victim of the crime or to his family. The same principle is followed in the 'Dooms' of Aethelberht, the first recorded English laws. Also, the King had evidently been influenced by his new advisers, the Christian bishops from Rome. For the opening paragraph of the 'Dooms' lays down the compensation to be paid in respect of church property or the property of priests. The church received very special protection; twelve times the standard compensation was to be paid for the theft of God's property and church property. A bishop's property attracted an elevenfold compensation, a priest's ninefold; and so on down to a simple clerk's, threefold. In the same way any breach of the church's peace or the peace of a place of assembly was punished by a fine of twice the usual amount.

The influence of the men from Rome, however, did not affect the fundamental form of the laws. First, they were written in English and not Latin. Second, there was no attempt to produce a comprehensive and logical code. Those who framed these dooms assumed that they were building upon a wide base of customary law, and that this law was well known and needed no re-definition. It was enough to say that a breach of the church's peace should be punished by twice the usual fine; there was apparently no need to record exactly what that fine was.

These laws show not only continuity with the ancient traditions as recorded by Tacitus, but also see the emergence of two important principles which were to persist and develop over the years.

First was the conception that wherever the king was present, wrongdoing was particularly heinous. No affray or unlawfulness should disturb the peace that surrounded the king's person. One of the laws laid down that 'If the King be drinking at a man's house and if a man should do anything wrong there, he shall make twofold compensation'. Even murder took on a special gravity if it was committed on one of the king's estates. 'If a man slay a man on the royal demesne, he shall make atonement of fifty shillings'. Gradually this idea of the special nature of the king's peace was to grow. Not in his presence merely, but throughout his realm, the peace of the king was to be preserved by all his subjects. This concept is still alive, and the sovereign's presence is, so to say, diffused throughout England in the persons of the judges and of the Justices of the Peace.

The second conception was that all the king's subjects, even the free men who had no masters, in some way belonged to him. The king was entitled to special compensation if a free man was killed, which threw the cloak of the king's protection over all free men. The position is clearly defined: 'If a man slay a free man, fifty shillings to the king for infraction of his right as lord'. Murder apart, when the free men of Kent were called up on the king's service, they enjoyed his particular protection. His business was not to be interfered with by private quarrels, nor was the number of his men to be diminished by injuries in private brawls. If anyone injured a man called up for service with the king, then he should pay twice the usual fine and, in addition, pay fifty shillings to the king. This was a considerable sum. In Kent the shilling represented the price of an ox: a fine of fifty times that amount would be a serious punishment for many and crippling for most.

For murder the punishment consisted of the payment to the dead man's family of 'man-money' or Wergeld. This amounted to one hundred shillings and was in addition to the money due to the king. It was sensibly recognised that it might take a man time to raise such a sum, so the law provided, then as now, that a criminal might be given 'time to pay': twenty per cent had to be paid forthwith and the balance in six weeks. It is incidentally interesting that the words of the law should echo the statement of Tacitus that the German tribes reckoned time by nights and not by days : 'If a man slay a man, he shall pay twenty shillings at the open grave and the whole Wergeld within forty nights'.

To enslave a free man was punishable by a fine of one-fifth of the fine for murder, namely twenty shillings.

The free men referred to in these laws were the *ceorls* or churls. Although the word has suffered degradation down the ages, its original meaning was noble enough. The churl was a freeborn farmer, having no lord except the king, who protected his life and his liberty. His servants were also protected; for the man who slew a churl's servant had to pay a Wergeld of six shillings. The churl was probably the descendant of one of the warriors who had sailed with Hengist and who had been granted land in the early days of the settlement. He is the prototype of the yeoman, the free farmer who—within the law and subject only to his duty to his king—is master of his own fate and upon whom so much of Anglo-Saxon society is founded.

In Kent, between the churl and the slave stood the *laet*, whose Wergeld is given as eighty shillings, only twenty per cent less than that of the churl. There were apparently three classes of *laet* : the laws give sixty shillings as the Wergeld for the second class and forty shillings for the third class. The *laets* (who are mentioned only in the laws of Kent and not in any other English kingdom) were probably fairly well-to-do British peasants living on in the land of their ancestors. Although (taking the Wergeld as an index of their standing) the Britons had become second- and third-class citizens compared with the English, they still came under the protection of the law, neither utterly despised nor utterly dispossessed. Britons and Jutes, descendants of the old mixed population of Roman Kent and of the sailors of Pegwell Bay, were alike the subjects of the Kings of Kent, free under the law; all were part of the new Anglo-Saxon people.

Early English society was of course disturbed by other troubles than murder. Brawls and private fights, though resulting in nothing more serious than a bruise or the loss of a tooth, were an affront to peace and of them the laws of Aethelberht took solemn and sensible cognisance. The compensation for a punch on the nose was set at three shillings, and for a mere bruise a shilling. To disfigure a man by knocking out his front teeth was twice as bad as hitting him on the nose, for the fine was six shillings a tooth; for the canines it was four shillings, for the pre-molars three shillings; for the molars, which hardly show, it was a shilling—the same as for a bruise.

Perhaps some of the private discord and fisticuffs arose from over-indulgence in that drink they made from fermented grain— the beer which Tacitus noted and to which the Anglo-Saxon people have been so constantly devoted under many skies and in many landscapes. Their poetry records how deeply they slept when they had drunk, and they may have become correspond-ingly bellicose before coma crept upon them. What is known is that drinking, and the kind of dispute that grows naturally among a group of men sitting over full beer mugs, became the subject of an early law. Some eighty years after the days of Aethelberht, the laws of Kent were expanded and among the additions is the following :

> If, where men are drinking, one man seize the cup from another without provocation, he shall, in accordance with ancient custom, give a shilling to him who owns the house, six shillings to the man whose cup was seized, and twelve shillings to the king.

Clearly, the offence of swiping another man's beer was con-sidered a grievous one: nineteen shillings—the total of the penalty—was almost one-fifth of the price of a man's life. Speculation on the value of beer apart, this law gives useful information. First it shows that the king's peace had greatly extended since Aethelberht's time; it was to be maintained throughout the kingdom, within the houses of all his subjects. Also, the wording of this law shows that the conditions it lays down followed custom that could already be described as ancient; many of these early laws were merely the writing down of traditional practices and penalties.

This revision of the laws of Kent was made by Hlotheri and Eadric, joint Kings of Kent in about AD 685. The Frankish name of Hlotheri, great-grandson of Aethelberht, is a reminder that the royal house of Kent was linked by marriage with the Frankish kings on the Continent. It may well be that the people of Kent, and more probably the nobility, maintained close contact with the Continent. Gaul lies only twenty-one miles from the Kentish port of Dover. Meetings and intermarriage were likely, not only within the royal family but possibly among the nobles. That Kent boasted a hereditary nobility is clear from these new laws, which lay down that a man of noble birth had a Wergeld of three hundred shillings, a vast sum. Birth and not achievements conferred the title of nobility; but were these nobles the cousins of the king, descendants of royalty, or were they perhaps the descendants of those followers of Hengist who, under him, had held positions of authority and command?

The new laws also reveal that the men of Kent were accustomed to cross the Thames northwards into Essex and were buying property in the great walled city of London. For it was laid down that if a man of Kent bought any property in London, he should take two or three reliable churls to be his witnesses or else the reeve of the King's demesne. Since such purchases were considered worthy of a place in the laws they were presumably not infrequent. It could only have been trade and commerce that would have prompted the men of Kent to acquire property in London. The south-east corner of Britain, then as in the days of the Romans, was linked to the Continent of Europe by the exchange of goods, and London lay at the centre of this activity. Moreover, the fact that special witnesses were required for transactions in London suggests that the city was seen as a place apart, where title to property had some special conditions attaching to it. If Romano-British life was still continuing in London, and if its inhabitants, of British and overseas descent, were felt to be a different people from the Saxon folk who dwelt around it, there would have been good reason for this precaution.

The laws of Hlotheri and Eadric make clear that a man was responsible for the wrongdoings of his servants. Should a man's servant slay a nobleman, then the master had not only to yield up his servant, but he himself had to pay 'the value of three men'. In the case of the murder of a mere free man, then the penalty laid upon the master was the value of one man. This kind of responsibility was even held to exist for a man's guest, if the guest came from another kingdom and stayed for three nights. Should such a guest, 'be it a merchant or anyone who has come over the border', do harm to any one, then the host had to bring him to justice or himself pay the penalties. First, the conception seems to have been growing that all men had a duty to maintain the King's peace in any situation where they held authority. Secondly, merchants are specifically mentioned as possible guests. The Roman road from London to the ports of Kent (still known as the Old Kent Road) would have been a pathway for trade and traders. Men from both English and Continental kingdoms would have passed along it, seeking hospitality for a night or two; and the Kings of Kent intended that their subjects should require orderly behaviour from the travellers.

King Hlotheri died just before Ceadwalla seized the kingdom of Wessex, and it was his laws that governed Kent when it was overrun by the West Saxons. When Ceadwalla abdicated and travelled to Rome, Ine became King of Wessex, in AD 688; he too was directly descended from Cerdic. Quite early in his reign, certainly not more than six years after he succeeded, he drew up a set of laws for Wessex. The preamble to them conveys significant information about that kingdom in the late AD 600s.

First, Ine refers to himself as *Ic Ine, mid Godes gife Wesseaxna kyning* . . ., 'I Ine, by God's gift of the West Saxons, king . . .' He is thus King by the Grace of God. His authority is based not merely upon his prowess as a war leader or his royal descent; unlike his pagan forbears he is seen as drawing his power from God, through the church which he supported.

Next, among the advisers he lists as having helped him with thought and with learning to draw up his laws, he names his own father, Cenred. Clearly the crown of Wessex was not looked upon as being purely hereditary. Kings were selected from the descendants of Cerdic, but evidently the eldest of the line did not invariably inherit. That a king could have a father living, and one not in disgrace but thought worthy to head the list of royal advisers, is a clear reminder of the words of Tacitus : 'They choose their kings for noble birth'. Descent from Cerdic gave a man the right to be among those from whom the king was selected; but it gave him no right to the crown without the process of selection. The partly hereditary, partly elective kingship persisted for many centuries.

The preamble also gives the names of two bishops who assisted in drawing up the laws. One is Erconwald, Bishop of London—*Eorconwaldes mines biscepes*—'Erconwald my bishop', a phrase which brings home the growing sweep of West Saxon authority. London lay within the kingdom of the East Saxons, yet its bishop is now seen as a member of the Council of the King of Wessex, to whom he is 'my bishop'.

Finally, the preamble defines the purpose of the laws as being 'the holiness of our souls and the steadfastness of our kingdom'. Although Christianity had been with the English for less than a hundred years, it was already a dominant factor in the king's mind. Church and state were moving forward together.

Indeed many of Ine's laws are aimed directly at Church matters. First, it is laid down that all priests must righteously hold to right rules of conduct. After that, all folk are bidden to follow the laws. A wide range of topics is covered. All children had to be baptised : if a child died before baptism the father forfeited all that he possessed. No man should work on Sunday. The church was a sure sanctuary for anyone fleeing the death penalty. Fighting carried heavy punishments. A thief was fined, but if he and his household conspired to rob, then they all went into slavery. Men had to maintain their fences and keep their cattle from straying. Service with the king's army was compulsory and neglect of this was severely punished.

Most significant are the many references to the Britons living
in the kingdom. Ine laid down that the Wergeld of a Welshman
having five hides of land was to be six hundred shillings. By
'Welshman' the laws did not mean an inhabitant of Wales, but
a man of British descent. Five hides represented a considerable
holding, so again it emerges that among the Britons it was not
merely the poor peasant or landless fugitive who stayed on in
the Saxon kingdoms. Nor did the laws of Ine protect only the
wealthiest of them. The Briton who possessed one hide had a
Wergeld of a hundred and twenty shillings, and if he had but
half a hide, then the penalty was eighty shillings. Even the
landless Briton had a Wergeld of sixty shillings. There were also
Britons in the king's service; the Wergeld of any Briton who, as
a horseman, went on the king's errands was two hundred shillings. For the law to have taken cognisance of such horsemen, they
must have been fairly numerous. The Britons were famous for
their horses in Caesar's day and perhaps this skill survived.

The English love of the law, and of the good order which the
law ensures, is shown clearly in these dooms of King Ine of
Wessex. They gave protection to both Saxons and Britons dwelling within the kingdom. The distinction between the two folk
gradually became blurred. After a few generations a man's
remote origins would have been forgotten; marriage between
the two peoples would have been inevitable. So the later men
of Wessex, though their language, laws and society were all
English, were descendants of Englishman and Briton alike. The
laets of Kent are evidence for a similar process in the extreme
south-east.

After the bitter wars between Ceadwalla and Kent, Ine made
peace with his eastern neighbour. During that peace King
Wihtred of Kent drew up a further set of laws for that kingdom.
One of them, identical with one of Ine's codes, provides that any
man travelling through a wood off the highway must either
call out or blow his horn; otherwise he would be assumed to be
a thief and could be slain. This suggests that both kingdoms

had agreed on a method of putting down marauders and raiders on the borders. The laws of Wihtred also provide that a man killed while robbing should bear no Wergeld; in other words men were to be allowed to use force in the defence of their property, and killing a thief was no murder. Capital punishment is provided as a possible penalty for theft. A thief caught red-handed could, at the king's choice, be slain, or sold as a slave overseas, or go free by paying a sum equal to his own Wergeld. The fact that to be sold overseas was a possible punishment implies regular slave trade with the Continent. And not all the slaves who were shipped across the channel were legal cargo : King Ine had found it necessary to impose a penalty on any man who sold one of his own countrymen, slave or free, beyond the seas.

Laws were also being drawn up in the northern kingdoms of the Angles. In the eighth century a powerful king with the honoured name of Offa was ruling over Mercia, and brief and tantalising references to his laws are made in other documents. Though nothing is left of them, the fact that such laws were drawn up is evidence that it was not merely in the south that the English were defining and writing down their laws, and seeking an ordered and organised society. Throughout England it is clear that kings were not merely possessed of special powers and privileges; they also had duties towards their subjects.

One of the documents that mentions the lost laws of King Offa is the set of laws drawn up by Alfred the Great, King of Wessex who began to reign in AD 871. In the preamble, Alfred wrote : 'But what laws I found, either from the days of Ine my kinsman or of Offa, King of the Mercians, or of Aethelberht who first in England received baptism, those that seemed to me most just, I gathered them herein and the rest I rejected'. So Alfred of Wessex, descendant of Cerdic, turned not only to the laws of his predecessor and kinsman Ine, but studied the laws of Mercia and of Kent. The adoption by both Ine of Wessex and Wihtred of Kent of the same law to discourage raiders and robbers from skulking in the roadside woods may have indicated the beginning of a desire to give the separate kingdoms a set of common standards; but Alfred went further and deeper. There was a conscious attempt to provide a set of laws acceptable to all Englishmen. A total unity of all the regions was made easier, and perhaps inevitable, once the idea of a unified law had been adopted. The conquest and forceful absorption of one kingdom by another was not enough to create a united realm of England, with one people living together as equal subjects of one crown. The adoption of common customs and common rights and duties under the law, was an essential step along the path. The work of Alfred had immense consequences. From his day the history of English law is a continuous one and the history of England becomes something more than the history of Wessex or of Mercia. His work may indeed carry a lesson for modern times, and point to what is perhaps the only way of building those large political unities, and indeed that world unity which is becoming so increasingly necessary.

Alfred moreover was perpetuating the traditions of a king's legislative duties. The examples that he had followed and so vigorously renewed were to influence his successors, even those kings who were to come from overseas; and the establishment of a lawful society, and of a kingship that was itself bound by the law, was secured for England.

The first of his laws defined the basic prerequisite of such a society: 'At first, we lay down that what is most needful is that each man should strictly hold to his oath and pledge'. Exception is given for a man who under duress has made promises to do evil things—'to betray his lord or to support any unrighteousness'. But breach of a lawful oath was severely punished. The wrongdoer had to leave his property and his weapons with his friends and to be imprisoned for forty nights in the king's house; while he was a prisoner his kinsfolk had to furnish his keep, 'if he had no meat, or, his kinsfolk had no meat, then the king's reeve should feed him'.

So these laws began to reveal something of the means of enforcement, upon which the earlier documents were silent. The king would have many houses, as his will confirms. His property is beginning to be used as an instrument of the public good. His reeve is the local representative of the crown and the authority of the king is spread over the land through his deputies.

Moreover, these laws recognise and condemn some actions less crude than man-slaying, fighting and theft. Deeds which work against a settled society, without being mere violence against persons and property, are now held to be unlawful. The breaking of an oath was not the only act in this category; Alfred's law provided a brutal penalty for any man who made a public slander. If this were proved against him, 'no lighter thing shall he suffer than that his tongue shall be cut off', though the slanderer could buy himself out by paying his Wergeld.

The liberty and rights of the churls or free farmers were strictly safeguarded: 'If a man binds a free man who has no sin, he shall pay ten shillings. If he beat him, he shall make compensation with twenty shillings'. Nor could a free man be put in the stocks, or have his hair forcibly cut or shaved in mockery, or have his beard cut off like a priest, without the offender paying a penalty. The king here is seen as a defender of his subjects' rights even against their own lords. In earlier days the lord's rights had been almost as absolute as his man's loyalty. The loyalty remained and Alfred's laws did much to support and insist upon its continuance; but the lord's rights became limited by the law and had to be lawfully exercised.

The old days and the ancient traditions were not forgotten. The good order of society still depended upon a man's loyalty to his lord, as it had done in the times described by Tacitus. Alfred's laws embody and preserve these ancient values. Loyalty to a lord and the lord's duty to protect his man excused much. A man, said the law, might fight on the side of his lord without becoming liable to vengeance, if his lord be attacked; and so might a lord on the side of his man. This loyalty was greater than loyalty to kin: a man might fight on the side of a kinsman if that kinsman had been unjustly attacked, save only against his lord.

Other laws show a society in which merchants travelled and traded and in which men still scuffled and brawled. There are fines for headwounds, and for wounds one inch long above the hairline or on the forehead, and for the lopping of ears : it was still a rough society. But it was beginning to establish some values of good conduct, a sense of order, formalities before fighting, and an acceptance of a central authority.

Indeed, the subject could now call upon the king or the king's representative to see justice done. For if a man felt that he had been wronged, he was not to seek redress in fighting or quarrel; he was formally to beset the wrongdoer in his house, holding him there for seven nights. Then, if the wrongdoer peacefully surrendered and gave up his weapons, the aggrieved man was to summon the kinsman of the wrong doer, so that right might be done. But (and this is the new and significant matter) if the wronged man had not the force to besiege his foe, he was to ride to the alderman (the king's officer) and ask the latter for help. If the alderman would not help, the man was to ride to the king. Only when he had exhausted these lawful possibilities could he start fighting his enemy. The responsibility of the king and of his officials to guard the peace of the kingdom is clearly defined. Alfred's kingship was far more than the kingship of his predecessors. Not a war leader merely, though he was a great one, nor the loved lord of a devoted troop of followers; he was the guardian of all free men's rights, the maintainer of the peace and the guarantor of order and justice.

England found Alfred's laws good and acceptable. For when, two hundred years later, William of Normandy became king of England by conquest, he swore at his coronation to uphold not only the laws of Edward, his cousin and recent predecessor, but also the laws of Alfred. Clearly they had come to symbolise, in the minds of the people of England, their rights, their liberties and perhaps their national identity.

Other folk were to come to the island, the Danes and the Normans, and were to add their traditions and customs to those of the English. Both people made massive contributions to the laws of England. But the early English kings had already seen the value and importance of ordered government and of a set of clear and simple laws. The roots of English law are English, though there has been much grafting, and the grafts have been fruitful. The tradition that society's rules should be set down, and that kings themselves should exercise their power both through and within those rules is ancient. Tacitus shows the beginnings, nearly two thousand years ago—'nor have their kings unlimited or arbitrary power'. The early laws of the English kingdom show the formalisation of that tradition. And *Magna Carta* and the Bill of Rights show the same tradition, modified by time and by new environments, persisting from age to age.

VI

GOVERNMENT BY CONSULTATION

BEFORE the Angles, Saxons and Jutes came to Britain,
their ancestors had established a fairly formal system of
consultation between chiefs and people, between the rulers
and the ruled. 'About minor matters' wrote Tacitus, 'the chiefs
consult; about greater matters, all. But even those things which
are kept for the general opinion are fully considered by the
chiefs'.

Evidence for the existence and responsibilities of this system
is to be found in all the early English kingdoms. There, as society
grew more settled, as laws were formalised into written documents, assemblies were modified and their duties in the drawing
up and administration of the law became wider and more
formal. These were the bodies that could ensure that no king
exercised his powers without the advantage of consultation with
men drawn from many parts of his kingdom, nor without checks
on his power.

In the preamble to his laws (about AD 690), King Ine of
Wessex specifically recorded that he had reached his conclusions
after full discussion with a large number of his advisers. In
addition to taking the advice of his father and of his two bishops,
he discussed matters *mid eallum minum ealdormaninum*—'with
all my aldermen'—*ond thaem ieldstan witum minre theode*—
'and the chief wise men of my kingdom'. 'The wise men' was the
phrase commonly used to define the assembly consulted by the

Page 103: (*left*) Bronze head of the Emperor Hadrian (AD 117-138) found in the river Thames at London Bridge; (*right*) bronze head (probably of the Emperor Claudius) found in the river Alde at Rendham in Suffolk.

Page 104: (*above*) Coin portraits of: 1 Edward the Confessor, 2 King Harold, 3 William the Conqueror; (*below*) purse-lid with gold plaques inset with garnets and glass, from Sutton Hoo, Suffolk, 7th century AD.

kings and a usual form was *witan gemoot*, the meeting of wise men. Also consulted was *micelra gesomnunge Godes theowa*—'a great summoning of God's servants'. So landowner and fighting man, thane and alderman, bishop and priest, sat with the king to consider what laws were best for the stability of the realm and the salvation of men's souls. The Witan of King Ine was little different from the assemblies of the days of Tacitus, some six centuries before, when chiefs and priests consulted together on matters of importance to the tribe. Ine's words bridge the centuries between the gatherings of the tribes two thousand years ago in Germany and the debates and decisions of Westminster, of Congress, and of the other English-speaking assemblies today. Bishops, landowners and men from all corners of Britain still gather to advise the crown or the government of the kingdom; in the manner of King Ine, the monarch today makes enactments only by and with the advice of the Lords spiritual and temporal and of the Commons in Parliament assembled. The outward forms of the institutions are different. Their purposes are the same, and their methods have much in common. Government and law-making by consultation, an attempt to discover the views of the people through the voices of men from various districts, a working together of Church and State—all these are to be found, in however primitive a form, in the Witan; and all are to be found today in Parliament at its best.

The subtle balance of power between the king on the one hand and the people on the other has varied from reign to reign, according to the personalities of the kings and the courage, skill and obstinacy of their advisers. There have been kings who have sought to dominate the assemblies; there have been assemblies which have wrested powers from the king. But the conception that there should be a dialogue between king and people, that the people's representatives—however arbitrarily selected—should have the right to advise and influence the king, is a very ancient one. Loyalty to the ruler and conviction of a duty to comply with the laws are both reinforced when those who owe that loyalty and that duty have played their own part

G

in influencing the ruler and in establishing those laws.

Bishops may have been called into the assembly even earlier than the days of Ine. Some seventy years before (some time after AD 600) King Aethelberht of Kent, the first English king to become a Christian, had drawn up a code of laws. The first of these, as we have seen, was framed to protect church property, and there is some evidence that he took the advice of his clergy in his task of lawmaking. Bede also says that he made his laws 'with the consent of his Witan'. The composition of the Witan is not fully described, as it is in Ine's document. Nevertheless, Aethelberht's code has a special interest : the first recorded laws of an English kingdom, written down more than one thousand three hundred years ago, were not drawn up by the king alone, but with the consent of his assembly.

The fact that Christian priests and bishops were immediately brought into the assembly suggests that in the Witan of each of the earlier English kingdoms there was a place for the pagan priests, and that, when the religion changed, the old practice continued, seeming natural and proper, though with a difference. If this were so, then there was complete continuity with the days of Tacitus, who mentions the prayers with which the tribal assemblies opened and records that only priests had the right to inflict the punishments of death, imprisonment or flogging. Since the assembly was competent to try capital charges, the priests must have sat with the warriors and nobles in those tribal meetings. The Archbishop of Canterbury and his colleagues who sit in the House of Lords are thus the heirs to the priests of Woden and of Thor.

At least one early English kingdom provides direct evidence for a pagan priest playing a leading part in a discussion in the Witan. Thirty years after the conversion of Kent by Augustine, Northumbria was still pagan. King Edwin of Northumbria (AD 617-633) had married a princess of Kent and she took with her, to her new home, Bishop Paulinus to be her chaplain and to preach the new religion to Edwin. The latter remained long in doubt and, when challenged by Paulinus for a decision, replied that he was willing to adopt the new religion, but that first he would have to consult with his advisers and friends. Bede records this in Latin. Alfred, who translated the work into English, writes: *thaet he wolde mid his freondum ond mid his wytum gesprec ond getheat habban*—'that he wished with his friends and his Witan to speak and to take thought'. Obviously the tradition of consultation was already so deep-rooted that a king found it normal and necessary to discuss with his Witan the wisdom of changing his own religion. More to our purpose, when the Witan was called together and questioned by the king, the first man to reply was Cefi, the King's senior priest. (Cefi, by the way, was a robust and engaging character. Having decided that the Christian faith was superior to his former religion, he mounted a stallion and, spear in hand, charged and overthrew the statues of his old gods.)

Bede recounts in full the answer given to the king by one of his counsellors. This, in a sense the first recorded parliamentary speech in English history, is worth quoting in full, in the version given by Alfred's translation:

> Thus to me seems, O king, this present life of man on earth, in so far as the span is unknown to us: such as when you sit at a meal with your aldermen and your thanes in wintertime; and so your fire is flaming and your hall is warm, and it rains and snows and storms outside; there comes in a sparrow and quickly flies through the house, coming in through one door and going out through the other. Look! For the time that he is inside, he is not touched by the storm of the winter. But afterwards he is out of sight and, in the shortest space of time, he soon comes back from winter into winter. So the life of man is seen for a fairly short space of time. What went before or what comes after, we do not know. Therefore if this new learning brings any knowledge and any certainty, it is worthy that we should follow it.

Such imagery and rhetoric may not have been common in the deliberations of these councils. Topics as vital as a change in religion, and the casting aside of centuries-old beliefs did not frequently present themselves. More usual was the less dramatic but equally vital task of lawmaking.

King Wihtred of Kent, whose laws were noticed in Chapter V, drew up his dooms in consultation with his Witan and, in the words of the document itself, 'with the consent of all'. What was developing was not merely government by consultation but government by consent. It was in accordance with this doctrine that Edwin of Northumbria sought the views, and by implication the assent, of his Witan before changing his faith.

Sometimes the Witan had tougher tasks. Kings wore their crowns with the consent of the council and the latter had the power to depose. The *Chronicle* tells us that in AD 757 *Cynewulf benam Sigebryht his rices ond Westseaxna wiotan for unrhytum daedum, buton Hamtunscire*—'Cynewulf and the Witan of the West Saxons deprived Sigebryht of his kingdom for his unrighteous deeds, except Hampshire'. We do not know what arguments were advanced in that stern assembly twelve hundred years ago, nor whether there were any voices to defend Sigebryht, a king and a king of Wessex, against the charges brought by Cynewulf. The outcome showed that an English king could not reign without the consent of the council of the nation, and that though kings hold sovereign power, they hold it only so long as they enjoy the confidence and trust of those whom they rule. The balance is a subtle and delicate one; kings who have not understood it have been compelled, like Sigebryht, to give up their kingdom.

In the case of Sigebryht the Witan was merciful; he was permitted to hold Hampshire. But in his smaller kingdom he failed, as he had failed in Wessex itself. For after a while he slew a faithful alderman named Cumbra who had stayed with him longer than any other. So he was driven into the Weald and was there stabbed by a peasant who thus avenged the murdered alderman. Cynewulf was himself later slain by the followers of Sigebryht's brother. It was a violent and vengeful society, where murder begot murder and where feuds persisted. This very violence makes all the more remarkable the fact that Cynewulf, before resorting to armed force against Sigebryht, thought it necessary to pursue within the assembly the question of his 'unrighteous deeds'. The incident shows a general acceptance of the Witan's power, even over kings, and the desire, even in violent times, to act lawfully.

This power could be used not merely to depose kings but also to redress the kingdom's grievances. Many years later, in AD 1014, the people were sinking into despair under the misrule of King Aethelred—the notorious Ethelred the Unready. The Danes, against whom his great predecessor Alfred had prevailed after many preliminary disasters, were again ravaging the kingdom, storming city after city, and roaming at will over the countryside. Aethelred's attempt to buy them off with large bribes had proved fruitless. Irresolute, his former policy in ruins and his army powerless, he was threatened with having his power wrested from him by the battle-eager invaders. He first sought refuge in the Isle of Wight, then left his kingdom and went, more or less as a fugitive, to France.

In his absence, the Witan met together—an indication that by now the assembly did not derive its power solely from the fact that its members were the king's advisers, summoned by him to help him in his sovereign tasks. That they could meet without the king's presence suggests that they were beginning to acquire a separate existence and that an authority, independent of the king's power, was vested in them as a body corporate. They were becoming something more than a council, and, in the king's absence, embodied the sovereignty of England. The *Chronicle* records that the gathering consisted of clergy and laity alike, and that they took counsel together for the kingdom's good. It was decided that the king should be sent for.

That the Witan, however desperate the perils which beset the realm, should consider that it had the right to summon its own lord is a dramatic demonstration of the limitations and the realities of the king's authority. It is also a dramatic example of the power of the Witan to remonstrate with the crown and to seek the redress of grievances. When, later, this power came into the hands of Parliament it was neither as novel nor as revolutionary as some have supposed. It had grown naturally and organically out of the age-old right of the assembly to advise. Exactly when advice became mandatory, and when true authority (for all the politely submissive language used towards the king by assembly and by Parliament) passed to the Witan, is hard to establish. But by Aethelred's day the shift in the balance was beginning.

But the Witan does not seem to have been anxious to display its power nakedly, nor openly to appear to be stripping Aethelred of his sovereignty. He was still their lord, and the language of their summons to him, as reported by the *Chronicle* in AD 1014, was not defiant: 'no lord was dearer to them than their rightful lord', though this protestation was qualified with the words 'if only he would rule his kingdom more justly than he had done in the past'.

The king did not appear in person before his counsellors, but instead sent his son Edward to them. The latter, on his father's behalf, gave a full undertaking that old grievances would be redressed and that he would be a good lord to them. The wording of the *Chronicle* suggests that this undertaking was given in writing, for it contains a phrase that was normally used in the opening words of a letter: 'He bade greet all his people'. So the relationship between the king and his assembly was becoming a formal one. Written assurances of better government by the king became part of the English tradition. Two hundred years later King John gave a similar written assurance to the barons and bishops. Magna Carta—the Great Charter—overshadowed all others, but it was not altogether novel; it was a step, but by no means the first step, along the road from the tribal assemblies described by Tacitus to the sophisticated subtleties of modern government. The monarch and not the people is sovereign; yet the king takes account of the people's will, or the will of that section of them which is literate or politically conscious. The words of the king's counsellors are the words of subjects—submissive, respectful and obedient. But the words must be heeded or the king's authority vanishes. Three hundred and fifty years later, in the late fourteenth century, William Langland in his poem *Piers Plowman* was to remind a King of England that 'Migt of the communes made hym to regne'.

The Witan also concerned itself with church issues. The appointment of bishops had long been a matter for the king's decision. True, in the first missionary days the church itself had made such appointments; Augustine had named his own successor as Archbishop of Canterbury and men were appointed to bishoprics by their colleagues. But as early as AD 685, a mere eighty years after Augustine's death, the *Chronicle* records that 'King Ecgfrith had Cuthbert consecrated Bishop'; and in AD 785 Hygerberht was appointed Archbishop of Lichfield by King Offa of Mercia. This power of the king (himself no priest) to appoint bishops within his realm, gradually came to be exercised by and with the advice of the Witan. In AD 995 Aelfric was appointed Archbishop by 'King Aethelred and all his counsellors'. The close link between Church and crown had been early established. But because a king's powers were, from the earliest days, exercised in consultation with his counsellors, the relationship with the church extended from king to assembly.

The process which began in Kent spread over the whole land. As England became one kingdom, the Witan of the English kings included the higher clergy of the whole country, and dealt with every kind of church matter. It was this special and interdependent relationship of king, church and Witan that gave its own character to the development of the Church in England and gave to the assembly of the counsellors, among whom the bishops themselves were numbered (and are numbered to this day), rights and responsibilities in religious matters that are sometimes misunderstood and frequently resented. The establishment of a Church of England, independent of the power of any foreign bishop, presided over by the king exercising his authority with the advice of his clerical and lay subjects, was an inevitable outcome of the methods and attitudes handed down from the earliest days.

By the tenth century the Witan's power was thoroughly

established. It selected kings and advised on the appointment of bishops. It could summon a king and request the redress of grievances and better government. It discussed taxes and agreed to their imposition, and considered the steps to be taken for the defence of the kingdom. It heard from the king his intentions in regard to the foundation and endowment of monasteries, and its members were the official witnesses of the king's charters and deeds of gift.

The conquest of England by the Normans and the coming of a foreign king might have shattered all continuity, and the traditions of the Witan could have died with the English army at Hastings. But this was not so. William the Norman claimed to be the acknowledged heir of Edward the Confessor and thus the legal successor of Alfred and of Cerdic. He was therefore at considerable pains to demonstrate a continuity between the old institutions and his own. He undertook to uphold the laws of Alfred, by which Englishmen had so long learned to live, and to maintain the laws of Edward. Many of the king's reeves, appointed by Edward and confirmed by Harold, continued in office under William. The Witan continued, in the same form in which it had existed under the Saxon kings. In AD 1085 the *Chronicle* reports that William spent Christmas with his counsellors at Gloucester for weighty and thorough talks 'about this kingdom and how it was peopled and by what kind of men'. Even a foreign king, his authority reinforced by his own ruthlessness and by men's memory of recent conquest, found it wise to follow the old practice of rule by consultation.

Nor did three generations of foreign kings destroy the tradition. Henry I, William's grandson, summoned a council at Gloucester in AD 1123. The Chronicle records its composition, which was the same as that of the Witan of former times: 'All his bishops, his abbots and his thanes'. The rights and duties too were unaltered, for the king asked them to select an Archbishop of Canterbury, and undertook to take their advice on the matter. Democracy, within a stable and ordered society, was slowly evolving.

VII

WESSEX AND THE DANES

B Y the middle of the AD 700s the new land of the English appeared to be taking its final and stable shape. Christianity had spread outwards from Kent to all the English lands, a lively force toward unity. The new learning which Christianity had introduced into the English kingdoms had yielded an abundant harvest. Not for the last time renewed contact with Rome had caused a rebirth of the arts and of the basic qualities of civilisation. The conception of law was replacing the mere observance of custom. The reduction of the old customary laws into writing, and the analytical thought and care which this process demanded, were not the only results of the growing literacy, and of the setting up of centres of learning in churches and monasteries. Bede had completed in AD 731 his *Ecclesiastical History of the English People*, and had brought to bear a degree of scholarship and objective investigation that is surprising for so early an epoch. In two hundred and fifty years the savage warrior society built by the Anglo-Saxon invaders had produced cultivated and devoted scholars.

The kingdoms of Wessex, Mercia and Northumbria were emerging as the only important political powers, the other kingdoms sinking into dependence upon one or other of the three dominant kings, to whose territories they were finally annexed. It could be foreseen that the process would continue and that one King of England, foreshadowed by those earlier kings who had taken the title of *Bretwalda,* would come to reign over a united land. The diverse origins of the inhabitants were not forgotten. Bede lists them—English, Britons, Scots and Picts— each with their own language. He adds significantly, however, that there was a fifth tongue, Latin, in which the scriptures of the single religion were read and which united all the different people. But a new threat suddenly put into jeopardy the very existence and identity of the coalescent nation of the English.

The land was invaded by another wave of people. They were pagan, holding the Christian faith in contempt; and they had no interest in unity, seeing the land as open territory where each leader could by conquest establish his own kingdom. Like the Angles and Saxons of earlier days they were bent on booty, bloodshed and conquest.

The first shadow fell during the reign of King Beorhtric of Wessex, just over three hundred years after Hengist brought his three ships into Pegwell Bay. Beorhtric, a direct descendant in the male line of Cerdic, became king in AD 786. Wessex was now a great kingdom and Beorhtric's position was one of considerable power and splendour. Three years after his succession he married Eadburh, daughter of King Offa of Mercia. The marriage was an event of great importance. Not only was it designed to bring closer together the two kingdoms of Wessex and Mercia, but it united the two most ancient and aristocratic families of the Angles and the Saxons. Eadburh was a descendant of the now-legendary King Offa who had fought the famous duel by the river Eider; so now the blood of Offa and Cerdic came together and the royal house of Wessex could begin to be seen as the royal house of England. It was both a sign for the future and an occasion that linked living men with the great figures of ancient days. Yet the entry in the *Anglo-Saxon Chronicle* records the marriage but briefly and goes on to tell of a more violent and tragic event:

> In this year King Beorhtric took to wife Eadburh, daughter of Offa. And in his day came first three ships, and the King's Reeve rode to them and wished to lead them to the King's

town because he did not know who they were. And they killed him. And these were the first ships of Danes that sought the land of England.

Clearly the reeve was unaware that the Danes had come as pirates or as raiders. He did not face them with an army, and his summons to them to go with him to the king's town was no more than he would have required of any peaceful traders. The laws of Alfred show that merchants were required to bring before the king's reeve the men who would be travelling with them through the countryside, and the law probably recorded a well-established custom.

According to another account (that of Aethelwerd, who wrote his *Chronicle* in about AD 1000) the reeve was at the time in Dorchester, and the *Annals of St Neots* reports that the three ships had landed at Portland. In the comparatively stable society of Wessex, in which loyalty to a lord lay at the foundation of good order, and properly vested with the king's authority, the reeve would have ridden confidently down to the seashore, to be met with defiance, to be set upon by the Danish seamen, and to be left dead upon the sand, his authority defied and the king's name set at naught. The raid was sudden and soon over and nothing further happened which the *Anglo-Saxon Chronicle* thought worthy of recording. Yet the affair was seen as a portent. It was the first time, since the Angles and Saxons had themselves come into Britain, that any hostile ships had come to the shores of the island or any invaders had landed.

Just as the ships of Hengist had presaged a full-scale invasion extending over many years, so the three ships that came to harbour in Portland were the forerunners of many thousands which, during the succeeding centuries, were to bring army after army into England. These armies were to march and to harry from Cornwall to Northumbria, sacking and looting, burning and slaying, seizing at least half of England as their own and almost destroying the infant nation of the English. The derided corpse of the king's reeve was the first of many thousands of English corpses to lie in the countryside and towns of England.

Blood was to flow not only on contested beaches and on the fields of many battles; it was to sprinkle the paved floors of looted churches and the steps of desecrated altars. Yet in the

STEM POST OF VIKING SHIP (EIGHTH CENTURY)

end the invaders were absorbed. Men who came as raiders remained as settlers; sea-rovers left their ships and dwelt in the towns and farms of England. All became subjects of the English kings and a new vigorous strain was added to the Anglo-Saxon people.

Meantime, brief though the Portland raid may have been, the danger to England was swift to grow. A mere six years afterwards the *Anglo-Saxon Chronicle* notes a further attack, this time in the North. It describes terrible portents that appeared in AD 793, exceptional lightning flashes and fiery dragons in the air. 'And after that,' it continues, 'in the same year the harrying of the heathen miserably destroyed God's church in Lindisfarne'. The Danes, like the Saxons before them, were showing that men who sailed the sea could find a pathway wherever they wished and dared. They could sail down the Channel to land confidently and impudently at Portland, or across the North Sea to seize the treasure of Lindisfarne. Three years later in AD 796, an English monk named Alcuin, a Northumbrian, wrote from France to King Offa of Mercia :

> I was indeed prepared to return, with the gifts I have received, to you and to my country . . . But I do not know what I should do among my own people; for among them no one is secure, nor is there any profit in wise counsel. The most sacred places are laid waste by the heathen.

Already, therefore, the heathen Danes were raiding England north of the Humber in sufficient strength and with sufficient frequency to shake and terrify the inhabitants. What is more, the churches and monasteries ('the most sacred places') were already the chief targets of their attacks. It was perhaps no special spite against or hatred for the Christian faith that prompted them, but rather the splendour of the booty : the island's holiest places were also its richest. The bones of the saints were kept in jewelled reliquaries; crucifixes were enriched with gold, and altars shone with candlesticks of gold and silver. Kings and great aldermen had bestowed wealth and treasure upon the churches which were, moreover, inhabited by unarmed men who raised no barrier to Danish arrows or axes.

The new raiders, whom the English records class as Danes, were in fact from many lands of the North, from modern Norway as well as from Denmark. They were kin to the Saxons and Angles, sharing many of their traditions, with a language close to that of the English. They were indeed very similar to the Angles and Saxons of three hundred years earlier: but the English had gradually learned from the Britons that the whole of the island south of the Wall had once been a single land, and could again become one. Also, Christianity had renewed the island's contacts with Rome and had given the English a love of scholarship and of holiness; they had seen the monasteries of the Britons and had soon founded their own. The Danes had as yet learned none of these things. To them the battle-axe, the spear and the sword were the only instruments fit for a man's hand. The proper use for gold and silver was in the rings, necklets and bracelets of a war-chief, not in ornaments dedicated to an alien and crucified god. It was as though the English were confronted with the embodied ghosts of their own seafaring and piratical ancestors. The outcome lay in doubt for three centuries.

It was the kingdom of Wessex and the house of Cerdic that finally ensured the survival of England and its absorption of the Danes. King Beorhtric died as the ninth century dawned. His kinsman Ecgbryht or Egbert, who could also trace descent through the direct male line from Cerdic, succeeded to the kingdom. The mixed Wessex population of Saxons, Britons and the descendants of settlers and legionaries of Roman times, had become fully integrated and fully united under the now ancient royal line of Cerdic. Egbert, a man of vision and ambition, could see that the kings of Wessex might become rulers of all England. His predecessor's marriage had been a movement toward some alliance between Mercia and Wessex; but Egbert hankered for a surer and swifter unity—a task not for politics but for the sword.

Within a dozen years of his succession he decided to secure his western frontier. Somerset, no doubt still containing a large number of folk descended from the Britons, was part of the kingdom he had inherited. Westwards lay Cornwall, where the unconquered Britons were still an independent and separate people. Here, in part of the old kingdom of Damnonia, the Britons had maintained Roman order and Roman traditions long after the legions had left. Uther Pendragon, Ambrosius and Arthur, the three great champions of the Britons against the invading Saxons nearly four hundred years earlier, all came from Cornwall. Their legend was preserved there, and the Britons still defied and sometimes attacked the men of Wessex. Egbert gathered together his army and marched westward the whole length of the peninsula, harrying as he went. He neither occupied nor annexed the territory, content to demonstrate to the Britons the sharpness of his sword.

Mercia, Egbert's northern neighbour, was his only true rival. Some ten years after the harrying of Cornwall, Egbert fought a great battle against the army of Mercia on the north-west frontier of his kingdom at Ellendun, near Wroughton in Wiltshire. The *Chronicle* speaks of a great slaughter and the rout of the Mercians seems to have been complete. For King Egbert felt no need to keep his forces on the Mercian frontier, but immediately sent them, under the command of his son Aethelwulf, eastwards across his wide kingdom, through Sussex into Kent. They drove out the King of Kent, who fled northward over the Thames, and Kent accepted Egbert as king. Sussex and Surrey also fell to his assault, acknowledging that they had formerly been under the rule of Wessex and that he was their lord. In the same year the kingdom of the East Angles turned to him for protection. Encouraged by this alliance and perhaps to show their good faith to their new lord, the East Angles marched against Mercia. Still shaken by the rout at Ellendun, Mercia fell and its king was killed. Four years later Egbert again called out his army and himself marched against Mercia. This time he was not content with a mere frontier battle, but subdued the whole kingdom. In the same year he led his army to Dore in Derbyshire in a demonstration against the Northumbrians. They sent a delegation to him and offered him not merely peace but also submission.

Egbert of Wessex now controlled the two great kingdoms of Mercia and Northumbria as well as all the minor kingdoms of the Angles, Saxons and Jutes. He proudly assumed the title of

Bretwalda, Lord of Britain, the eighth man to do so since the coming of the English, and the first to give reality to the dream that there should be a single government, as there had been in Roman days, from the lonely Wall of Hadrian to the restless waters of the Channel. The year was AD 825, and Egbert was at the summit of power. He was Lord of Britain indeed, and a descendant of Cerdic was now in real truth King of England. Cerdic had secured for his descendants power over all the mixed population of his new land. They had now increased their inheritance (which they still possess) to include the crown of all England.

The threat of the Danes demanded a strong and central authority in the island and Egbert achieved his wide powers just in time. He and his descendants were able to ensure that the new invaders did not destroy the fabric of the new land, but were to merge fully with the Anglo-Saxon people and to become in the end the subjects of the English crown. For a time, despite Norse raids on Northumbria, the south was quiet and Egbert pursued his ambition of a united Britain. In AD 830 he took his army into Wales and brought the Welsh into submission.

Then, four years later, the Danish ships entered the estuary of the Thames. Their bulwarks gay with painted shields, their dragon beaks, thrusting towards the heart of England, the adventurers came to land on the Isle of Sheppey in Kent. There they pillaged and slaughtered, ransacked and looted, and the south now had a bitter taste of what the north had so long endured. Next, no fewer than thirty-five Danish ships swept up the Channel and landed at Carhampton in Somerset. This was the first attack in strength upon the territory of Wessex itself. Egbert marched against them but was defeated in a battle of great slaughter. Wolf and raven, hawk and eagle, feasted upon the dead. The Danes, learning something of the politics of the west country, next saw the opportunity of breaking the power of Wessex by inciting the Britons to war. They therefore sent a large fleet into Cornwall and marched with the Britons against the English. But Egbert forestalled them and successfully combated their forces at Hingston Down in Cornwall; Britons and Danes were put to flight.

For the next ten years the Danish raids continued and increased. There were landings at Southampton and Portland, in Lincolnshire and in Kent, and in East Anglia. The Danes again came up the Thames and this time stormed the walled city of London. They achieved what the Saxons are never recorded as doing, and the stout Roman walls did not defeat them. The Norsemen sailed up the Medway and took Rochester, another city protected by Roman fortifications. Such triumphs demonstrate that the Danes and Norsemen were coming in vaster numbers than the Angles and Saxons had done when they themselves first began their invasion; the *Chronicle* speaks of thirty-five ships on one raid, of thirty-three on another. Whole armies were now being transported and isolated raids were merging into full-scale war.

In AD 851 came the terrible climax. A huge fleet of three hundred and fifty ships came to the mouth of the Thames. There had been no assault on this scale since the Roman invasion. Again the Danes stormed London, driving back the Mercian army that opposed them. They made landings on the south bank of the Thames and entered Surrey. They marched to Canterbury and took it—the capital of Kent, England's oldest kingdom. The city where Christianity had been first planted among the English was occupied by the heathen host. They sent a great army southwards by sea to Sandwich, but there they were defeated by Aethelstan of Wessex, the King of Kent, and nine of their ships were taken. Now, for the first time, the army of the Norseman did not sail away after the harrying, taking their booty back to the fjords and havens of their own country. They beached their ships and insolently stayed the winter through on the Isle of Thanet, the very place where Hengist's men had first settled. The new struggle for possession of the island had begun.

The independent Britons of Wales, heartened by the news of England's difficulties, rose against Mercia. King Aethelwulf of

H

Wessex, who had succeeded his father Egbert on the latter's death in AD 839, sent help in answer to Mercia's appeal, and his armies marched into Wales and reimposed his authority there. Wessex was thus beginning to be recognised as the protector of all England. To mark the alliance and to renew the friendship between the two royal houses, the King of Mercia married a daughter of Aethelwulf. Meantime an army drawn from the dependent kingdoms of Surrey and Kent sought to dislodge the Danes from Thanet; the engagement was inconclusive and many men died on both sides.

King Aethelwulf was a pious man. Towards the end of his reign he gave a tenth part of his estates to the church, and also visited Rome, remaining there for twelve months. Earlier he had sent his younger son, Alfred, on the same journey : in Rome the young prince was confirmed by the Pope and saw something of the learning and splendour which still survived in the Eternal City.

When Aethelwulf died, he was succeeded by his son Aethelred who continued the struggle against the Danish host. Alfred, the new king's brother, was with him throughout his campaigns, sharing responsibility and danger. The Danes were now settling in Britain and a huge Danish army was permanently under arms in the island, roving almost at will. In AD 867 the kingdom of Northumbria fell to a host that had marched northwards over Humber and had taken the city of York. In the same year the Danes invaded Mercia in force and seized Nottingham. The king of Mercia again appealed to Wessex for help. King Aethelred and Alfred marched to Nottingham but there was no engagement, for the Mercians had made their peace with the Danes who withdrew into York. When the winter was over the Norsemen again marched and the whole of East Anglia fell to them.

With Northumbria and East Anglia gone, with Mercia under threat, Wessex stood almost alone. But neither King Aethelred nor his brother weakened in their resolution. In AD 871 the Danish army was thrusting against the eastern frontier of their kingdom, and came to Reading. There, after a skirmish with one of the king's deputies, they were attacked by Aethelred and Alfred. The men of Wessex were defeated, but they withdrew in good order and seemingly in good heart. A mere four days later they attacked again. The battle went on till nightfall and this time the English were victorious. A fortnight later, at Basing, fourteen miles away, the Danes won. Yet another engagement took place a little later, and again the English were driven from the field after an initial victory. The number of battles fought, the return to the attack time after time—although their army had been mauled and beaten by the Danes and several of their leaders killed—speaks of an obstinate and dogged courage. Not for the first and certainly not for the last time, an English army was withstanding disaster and defeat without loss of hope and without dimunition of belief in final victory. Weary with marching, their sword-arms stiff, suffering defeat after defeat at the hands of ruthless enemies, the armies of Wessex continued in the field as an effective and indeed aggressive fighting force. The Danes, even in their moments of triumph, as they leaned breathless upon their spears at nightfall, the ground thick with English dead and the forces of Wessex in retreat, must have felt a chill of despair. As they flexed their muscles they must often have wondered, self-confident as they were, whether they could ever finally gain the victory. Fresh reinforcements came to the Danes that year from their own lands, and they resolved to finish with the men of Wessex.

Then, in the spring of the year, just after Easter, when the disputed Wessex hills and farms were at their greenest, Aethelred died. The time was critical for Wessex. The Danish army, reinforced, was poised to complete the conquest of the kingdom. Although Aethelred left sons, they were still children and this was no time for a child to wield the sceptre; the Witan therefore chose his brother Alfred as king. Now in his late twenties, the latter assumed command of the armies which he had so often led as his brother's lieutenant.

His reign opened in defeat and disaster. While he was attending his brother's funeral at Wimborne, the English force left to guard Reading was attacked and defeated. Later he himself, with a small company, marched against the Danes at Wilton, only to be beaten back. During this terrible year the men of Wessex fought no fewer than nine pitched battles against the Danes, and sent out numerous raiding columns, commanded by Aethelred or Alfred, or by one of their aldermen or thanes, to harry and to harass the Danish host. On the Danish side a king named Bagsecg was killed, and nine jarls or war-leaders. The remaining Danish king, Halfdene, withdrew from Wessex and took up winter quarters in London. His grip on the city was complete; from its mint he even issued pennies and halfpennies bearing his initials. Winter over, he led his host northwards to Northumbria, and Wessex had some respite. Mercia was again attacked and its king abdicated, spending the rest of his life in Rome. In his place the Danes set up a puppet king, who was compelled to allow them to use Mercia as a base for their further wars.

The Danish host was now large enough to separate into two distinct armies. One, under Halfdene, remained in the north; the other, under a king named Guthrun and two other kings, marched southwards to Cambridge. Halfdene's men settled in what is now Yorkshire, taking land there permanently as farmers and as the lords of large estates. The *Anglo-Saxon Chronicle*, under the year AD 875, reports that Halfdene shared out the lands of Northumbria and that his men busied themselves in ploughing and earning their living. Guthrun's men in AD 876 once more invaded Wessex, by now the only English kingdom not under the power of the Norsemen. They occupied Wareham and laid waste the country round about.

Alfred was compelled to seek peace. But with his army still in the field and with the reputation he had won for military skill and unconquerable resolution, he was able to make peace as an equal. He paid a sum of money to the Danes, it is true; however they on their side undertook to withdraw from Wessex forthwith. They swore to this treaty upon the sacred armlet of their king—a particularly solemn form of oath which before they had given to no man. Wessex, which had stood out for eighty years, won a respite. But the peace was short-lived, and the war was renewed in the following year. Although Alfred had set an army to watch King Guthrun's host, the Danes slipped quietly from Wareham by night and, despite their solemn oath, rode into Exeter and occupied the city. One hundred and twenty ships set sail to bring them reinforcements, but fate was now on the side of Wessex and the ships were lost in a storm off Swanage. Alfred rode to Exeter and pent up the Danes. They did not offer battle but gave him hostages, renewed their oaths, gave peace to Wessex, and then rode northwards into Mercia; again Wessex seemed secure.

In AD 878, however, in the depth of winter, they returned and occupied Chippenham, from this base raiding far and wide through Wessex. The English army was defeated and their territory occupied. Many of them fled as refugees to the continent. Alfred, with a small following, retreated through the woods and marshlands in the west of the kingdom. It seemed that Wessex had at last been overwhelmed. But even now, with the king no more than the leader of a small and fugitive army, the resolution of Wessex did not falter. When a fleet of twenty-three ships came during the same winter into Devon under Halfdene's brother, Alfred's men rallied and fought them. In the battle the Danish leader fell with over eight hundred of his men.

During that winter of AD 878 the fortunes of Wessex ebbed to their lowest. But with the spring, hopes renewed. Alfred built a fortified headquarters on the Isle of Aethelney in Somerset and gathered about him a new army from the men of that region. In early summer he rode out of Aethelney and encamped near Selwood. Then, says the *Chronicle*, 'there came to him all the men of Somerset and Wiltshire and that part of Hampshire which was on this side of the sea and they rejoiced to see him'. Wessex had her king again and her king once more had an army.

With this army he marched to Iley and thence to Edington,

THE DANES IN ENGLAND
ABOUT 880 A.D.

BERNICIA

NORTH
SEA

Isle of Man

IRISH   SEA

DANISH
NORTHUMBRIA
York

DANISH
MERCIA
Lincoln

Chester

The
Wash

Nottingham
Derby
Stamford
Leicester

WALES

KINGDOM
OF
MERCIA

THE LANDS OF
GUTHRUN

London

Thames
Estuary

Bristol Channel

KINGDOM
OF
KENT

KINGDOM OF WESSEX

Winchester

CORNWALL

Isle of Wight

where he attacked and finally routed the Danes under Guthrun, having besieged them in their base for two weeks. The Danes once more gave him hostages and renewed their oaths to leave the kingdom in peace; Guthrun and twenty-nine of their leaders agreed to be baptised, the ceremony taking place near Aethelney. Guthrun spent twelve days with the triumphant Alfred who celebrated the treaty by giving him costly presents. Wessex had been saved and with it the whole of England.

Within a few years Alfred had resumed his position of protector of the whole land. He occupied London in AD 886 and set one of his aldermen in charge of the liberated city. In the same year the *Chronicle* reports that 'all the English people submitted to him save those who were in captivity to the Danes'. So a bare nine years after his retreat to Aethelney he was once more King of all England, albeit an England still beset. For the assaults of the Danes continued, with new landings in the South. Alfred fought them in Kent and in Devon; their main army took Chester and there stood secure behind the old Roman walls. There was fighting in East Anglia and in Northumbria, and the Danish fleets sailed again to Wessex. But Alfred had built ships and fought them at sea.

Alfred had to accept that there was no question of expelling the very large Danish population which was firmly settled in East Anglia, eastern Mercia and Northumbria. The boundaries between the two peoples were agreed: first the Thames, then the Lea to its source and so to Bedford, then up the Ouse to Watling Street. Danes and English were to be equal before the law and the *wergeld* of a free Dane was to be the same as that of a free Englishman.

Alfred died in AD 901, leaving much to be done by his successors and many battles to be fought. England was to pass under the rule of Danish kings and later many may have felt that the cause which Alfred defended had been lost. But he had succeeded fully in his task and his work endured. Had the Danes conquered Wessex, the identity of England and of the Anglo-Saxon folk would have been lost. Learning might have died utterly from the land, books and manuscripts smouldered in the burnt ruins of the monasteries. The Danish host would have founded many kingdoms as each war-leader sought to establish himself as a king. A new dark age would have engulfed the island, its people lost in the tide of invaders. In preserving Wessex and in maintaining the continuity of English rule, Alfred ensured that the Danes saw themselves in the end as dwellers in England and as an integral part of the nation they had come to conquer.

All that we know of Alfred is impressive: his high courage and long patience in war, his refusal ever to admit defeat, and the speed with which he recovered his position as leader of all England after being driven to the Isle of Aethelney. Skill and courage in war were only part of his many achievements. We have seen how with his Witan he collected the laws of Wessex, Mercia and Kent, drawing up a new code that would be acceptable to all, and would be a symbol of and an influence towards the unity of the separate kingdoms. In spite of his many battles, he found time to attend to all the details of his country's government. He wrote tirelessly so that learning might be preserved. He translated Bede's history from Latin into English; he translated Pope Gregory's *Cura Pastoralis* and the works of Orosius. He sent a letter to each of his bishops exhorting them to foster learning, and ordered that all the sons of free Englishmen should, if they had the means, go to school and be educated in the English tongue. He made notes of the voyages of exploration made by two sea-captains. The tradition of the soldier-scholar is strong in England, and Alfred was one of the first to set the pattern.

He was long remembered and long loved. Men called him 'England's darling' and his wisdom and justice were recalled in succeeding ages. More than any other single person he secured the future of the Anglo-Saxon people. Briton, Roman, Angle, Saxon, and Jute had come together; Alfred's delaying action made it possible for the Norsemen and the Danes, the tough and freedom-loving seamen from the lands of the northern seas, to fuse with them.

VIII

THE DANISH KINGS

A T first Alfred's triumph seemed permanent. His son
Edward who succeeded him was a great war leader,
who maintained the position of Wessex as the protector
of England, and brought the whole land under his sole sway.
During the twenty-four years of his triumphant reign he led his
armies victoriously through the length and breadth of England.
He fought the Danes, both the resurgent settlers and the new
invaders, in Mercia and East Anglia. He marched north to
Nottingham, Bakewell, Manchester and Stamford. Realising
that the Danes had gained many victories by their policy of
seizing the main cities, he organised the rebuilding of the fortifications of many of the towns. The Danish host centred on
Cambridge recognised him as their lord, as did the Danes settled
in East Anglia; the *Anglo-Saxon Chronicle* claims that three
kings of the Britons in Wales, together with all the Welsh people,
gave him allegiance; the whole of Mercia and of Northumbria,
English folk and Danish settlers alike, accepted him, receiving
him as 'father and lord'. Edward the Elder was truly king of the
whole English nation and most effectively held his great inheritance. By the time of his death in AD 924, the Danes who had
settled in England were no longer aliens seeking to set up their
own kingdoms, but were the acknowledged subjects of the
English king, and it seemed that the danger to England was at
an end. Yet thirteen years later his successor Athelstan again

had to fight the invaders and won the battle of Brunnanburgh, the subject of the poem from which quotations have already been given. The battle was a triumph :

There by Brunnanburgh,   they broke the shield-wall
Hewed the hard linden bucklers   with hammered swords,
The sons of Edward,   as their inheritance is,
Which they are born to;   that they in battle often
Against the loathed enemy   the land should defend,
Hoarded wealth and homes. . . .

The victory was won over a combined army of Scots and Danes. These Danes were not rebellious settlers, but a new wave of adventurers who had come with their leader Anlaf over the sea to seek their fortune and to meet their fate in the fight. Five of their young kings were left dead on the battlefield, cut down by English swords; seven of Anlaf's earls also fell, with an uncounted number of sailors and Scotsmen. Once again the descendants of Cerdic, 'the sons of Edward', had preserved their land and homes. But the new invasion was a portent of future defeat; the five young kings and Anlaf's other followers were the precursors of many thousands who were to sail from Norway and Denmark as raiders and destroyers.

In AD 940, forty years after Alfred's death, Aethelstan died. Edmund, only eighteen years old, succeeded him and was at once faced with renewed attacks. The five great boroughs of the midlands—Leicester, Lincoln, Nottingham, Derby and Stamford —were in the hands of the Norsemen, who had held them for many years and within them, although from time to time acknowledging the sovereignty of the English kings, had maintained considerable political independence. They had more than once caused Mercia to rebel against the king's authority, and the five boroughs were an effective barrier between Northumbria and the might of Wessex. Behind this shield Northumbria now invited Anlaf the Dane to come from his settlement in Ireland to be their king. Young Edmund marched against Mercia and captured the five boroughs; the Danes of Mercia, descendants of an earlier generation of settlers, saw this as an act of liberation, freeing them from the tyranny of the Norsemen. Anlaf barely escaped from the siege of Leicester and all Mercia came once more under the power of Wessex. Northumbria was recovered shortly afterwards and the two Danish kings, Anlaf Sihtricson and Raegnald Guthrifson, were driven out. Edmund died in his early twenties after a brief but brilliant reign.

Fighting continued in the north. A Norseman, Eric Bloodaxe, had set himself up as an independent king in the city of York, which the Danes had held for close on a hundred years. It was not until AD 954 that the Northumbrian English drove Eric from his kingdom; his memory has been preserved in two Icelandic poems. One, *The Saga of Egil son of Skallagrim*, gives an account of his death. Odin hears the sound of a great army of men, slain in battle, approaching Valhalla. He knows that it is Eric and sends two of his most famous warriors to greet the newcomer. 'Welcome! What heroes come with you?' they ask. 'Five kings' proudly answers the ghost of Eric; 'I will tell you their names. And I myself am the sixth'.

There followed twenty tumultuous years, with new waves of invaders coming from Norway and Denmark, and with the kings of Wessex precariously maintaining their hold upon the land.

King Edgar who had succeeded to the kingdom in AD 959 died sixteen years later, leaving two sons, Edward and Aethelred. The former was a stern man who inspired fear and terror. According to the monk who wrote a *Life of St Oswald*, there were many who would have preferred as king the younger son Aethelred, mild and gentle both in word and deed, but Edward was finally chosen. A few years later, when visiting Aethelred, he was assassinated. If the biographer of St Oswald is to be believed, it was men of Aethelred's own household who comitted the murder, surrounding Edward in ostensible welcome as he rode up to the house, offering him wine and then stabbing him. He was long remembered as Edward the Martyr and the *Chronicle* in recording the murder says that:

No worse deed was ever done among the English since first they came to the land of Britain. Men murdered him but God raised him up. In life he was an earthly king. But now, after death, he is a heavenly Saint.

Suspicion must fall upon Aethelred the mild-mannered. He became king in his brother's place and there began one of the most disastrous reigns that England has ever suffered.

The very next year, AD 980, the sea-borne invaders again struck. Some stormed Southampton, slaughtering or enslaving most of the inhabitants. Some ravaged the Isle of Thanet. Others sailed up the river Dee and attacked the once-prosperous city of Chester, whose stout Roman walls proved of no avail. In the years that followed, fleets of raiders made landings in Devon, Cornwall and Dorset. Watchet was ravaged and the king's representative in Devon was killed. In AD 993 another Anlaf, who was later to become King of Norway, came with a fleet of ninety-three ships to Folkestone, harried the countryside and sailed on to Sandwich. Thence his army marched to Ipswich and so on to Maldon in Essex, where they were met on the river Blackwater by Byrhtnoth and his East Saxon troops. There, as seen in the poem 'The Battle of Maldon', quoted in Chapter I, Byrhtnoth fell and all the men of his house fought till they died to avenge their dead lord.

In this year of disaster, when it appeared that the century of struggle had proved vain, and when the cause of Wessex and of England seemed lost, King Aethelred decided to seek peace by buying off the Danish host 'because' as the *Anglo-Saxon Chronicle* puts it, 'of the great fear which they had caused all along the sea-coast'. The Danish host was paid the then huge sum of ten thousand pounds. As was to be expected, the payment merely stimulated further attacks. When gold could be bought not with blood and blows but by sailing across the seas and doing no more than threatening the weakened realm of England, the interest of the Norsemen rose and the raids increased.

King Aethelred, perhaps remembering Alfred's use of a fleet to stop the Danes at sea, called his Witan to consider how best to organise English sea power. He and his counsellors ordered that all ships in good trim should be brought to London. The command was given to Aelfric, one of his aldermen, jointly with two bishops and another soldier. Aelfric proved a traitor, warned

DANISH HELMET

the Danish fleet, and went over to the enemy. The Danes landed in East Anglia and approached London, to be stoutly resisted. The host then sailed north to the Humber and harried the countryside. The Northumbrian leaders fled and their armies followed them. London was besieged again, but the attackers were beaten off. Finally, three years after the decision to buy peace, King Aethelred invited Anlaf, who was again raiding, to meet him at Andover, promising him gifts. There the Danish leader was baptised, the king himself standing sponsor. Aethelred seems to have been consciously following the example of Alfred, who had similarly arranged for the baptism of Guthrun. He

was partially successful, for Anlaf kept his oath never to go raiding in England again, but sailed away in peace—the richer by
sixteen thousand pounds in gold and silver. For that was the
price paid by Aethelred for Anlaf's promise—and perhaps for
his baptism!

The tenth century ended with the Danes ranging the English
Channel at will. The men of Devon again saw the terrible
longships sweeping into the shore, moving smoothly and sweetly
over the water, sails set and oars flashing in the sunlight. There
was slaughter in Cornwall and in Wales. Watchet was harried
again and there was burning and killing. The ships sailed south-
about past Land's End, up the mouth of the Tamar and on to
Tavistock and Lydford, burning the farms and slaughtering the
people. The Isle of Wight was occupied and the horn-helmeted
warriors foraged throughout Hampshire and Sussex. Kent was
invaded and the Danes sailed along Thames and Medway. As
English armies were put to flight, the misery of despair and
defeat spread throughout the kingdom. In the last year of the
century the harassed king and Witan resolved to organise both
a navy and a land-force. But all things went awry so that neither
came to anything and, as the *Chronicle* bitterly noted, the only
result was 'toil for the people, waste of money, and encourage-
ment for the enemy'.

In the year AD 1000 Anlaf, now known as Olaf, King of
Norway, was defeated by King Sweyn of Denmark in a great
naval battle in the Baltic. The tale is told in the *Heimskringla*.
Olaf, with only eleven ships, was attacked by Sweyn and two of
his allies. Olaf refused to retreat and finally leapt overboard,
preferring death to capture. Sweyn of Denmark was now master
of the seas and under his leadership the raids of the Danes on
England increased. Frequently and vainly King Aethelred offered
them tribute: in AD 1012 they received forty-eight thousand
pounds. In the same year they killed Aelfeah, Archbishop of
Canterbury, pelting him with beef bones in a drunken festival
of violence because he had refused to pay them money.

King Sweyn came again and landed at Sandwich, then sailed

north to Humber and Trent. The men of Danish descent who dwelt north of Watling Street (the frontier drawn in Alfred's treaty) submitted to him, under compulsion feeding his army and providing horses. Then he gave command of the army to his son Cnut, and the host crossed Watling Street and rode south as far as Oxford and Winchester where Alfred lay buried. Both towns were taken. King Aethelred was besieged in London but escaped before the city fell. After seeking refuge in the Isle of Wight, he fled overseas to France, where he had already sent his two sons for safety. In the following year Sweyn died and Aethelred returned, having first, as we have seen, been summoned by the Witan who were resolved that on his return there should be better government and more effective resistance.

But Cnut the son of Sweyn was as relentless as his father. He sailed south from Lindsey, landed in Sandwich and put ashore the English hostages whom his father had taken, having first cut off their hands and noses to mark his contempt for his foes. Aethelred again bought peace with a further twenty-two thousand pounds. Two years later, in AD 1016, Cnut brought one hundred and sixty ships, sailed up the Thames and ravaged Mercia. Edmund, Aethelred's son, raised an army and marched north. But Cnut evaded him, turning south. On St George's day Aethelred died and Edmund was appointed king by the citizens of London and such of the Witan as were there.

Not for nothing did Edmund win the nickname of Edmund Ironside. He slipped out of besieged London and rode into Wessex where the people acclaimed him and where he fought two pitched battles that same summer. He raised an army in Wessex and liberated Kent. Finally he overtook the Danes in Essex and fought them at Ashingdon. But, in the words of the *Anglo-Saxon Chronicle*, 'Cnut won the victory and with it all England'. There was great slaughter among the English and Edmund retreated into Gloucestershire. Thither went Cnut with his hosts and the two kings met at Alney. They made peace on the basis that Edmund should be king of Wessex and Cnut king of Mercia. But in November Edmund died and Cnut the Dane became king of all England. It was two hundred years since the first Danes had landed at Portland, flouting the king's authority and killing the king's reeve.

But the long struggle of Wessex had not been in vain. For within two years of Cnut's accession the English and the Danes met at Oxford and agreed together that all should follow the laws of Edgar. So Cnut the Dane became heir to the English laws and traditions of Wessex. Thanks to Alfred and to his successors, the Danes carved out no new kingdom in the island of Britain. There was to be no foreign people set among the surrounding English. Cnut was king of a united England; indeed he was the instrument through which the work of Alfred was completed. For the Danes, both the new men and the descendants of the earliest settlers, were content to be subjects in a land where a Danish king could rule, and content to adopt the laws of their English neighbours.

Cnut reaffirmed the decision taken at Oxford that the laws of Edgar should be followed, and he ruled England as it had long been ruled, consulting his bishops and his subjects. He even travelled to Rome and negotiated with the Pope on behalf of all, English and Danes. After twenty years as king of England he died at Shaftesbury in AD 1035 and was buried at Winchester, the old royal city of Wessex where Alfred lay. He left two sons: Harold Harefoot, his illegitimate son by an English mother, and Harthacnut, who was living in Denmark.

Twenty years under a Danish king had not impaired the continuity of England's institutions. Shortly after Cnut's death the Witan met at Oxford to decide the succession. The men from London and all the thanes north of the Thames chose Harold Harefoot; Godwin, leader of Wessex, chose Harthacnut and a compromise was reached. Harold Harefoot was declared protector of England for himself and Harthacnut. The latter's mother, Emma, was to dwell under the protection of Earl Godwin of Wessex, living in Winchester with Harthacnut's house-troops about her, holding all Wessex in her son's name. She was sister to the Duke of Normandy, had once been Aethelred's queen and was the mother of his two sons—Edward and Alfred (named after his great ancestor). On Aethelred's death she had married Cnut to whom she had borne Harthacnut.

Her two sons by Aethelred were still living in France where they had taken refuge. The younger, Alfred, came to England to see his mother in Winchester, thinking that the troubled times were over. But Godwin did not dare to permit a prince of the house of Cerdic to appear in Wessex; the people might have flocked to him, as they had for six hundred years flocked to his ancestors, and Godwin's greatness depended upon his ruling Wessex in the name of Harthacnut. So he seized the young prince and blinded him, and Alfred lived out his life as a sightless monk at Ely, dreaming perhaps of the Wessex sword he might have wielded and of the Wessex crown he might have worn.

When Harold Harefoot died at Oxford in AD 1040, Harthacnut sailed over from Denmark with a great fleet to Sandwich and took the kingdom. He was received joyfully both by the English and the Danes. Aethelred's other son Edward, was biding his time, no doubt filled with hatred for Godwin and his men. He remembered also his own mission to England on his father's behalf, to answer the summons of the Witan, and to convey his father's assurances of better government. He had learned that high descent was not enough to obtain power in England. The old kingdoms had sunk into mere earldoms under a single crown. Godwin as Earl of Wessex sat in Edward's chair and the prince, who had greater ambitions than to be a mere earl in the land his ancestors had ruled, knew that he must be patient.

Then, when Harold Harefoot died, he felt his time had come. Harthacnut, in whose name Godwin ruled in Wessex and who was now King of England, might protect him; Harthacnut and he were after all half-brothers. So Edward came to live at Harthacnut's court, and the seed of Cerdic was again close to the throne of England.

Harthacnut in fact reigned only for a year, dying suddenly

I

in 1041 at Lambeth. He was a vindictive man and, according to the *Anglo-Saxon Chronicle*, 'never did anything worthy of a king'. He even had the dead body of his brother, Harold Harefoot, exhumed and thrown into a marsh. Edward, son of Aethelred, who had been living quietly in his household, was duly acclaimed as king. For twenty-four years England had been governed by Danish rulers. During this period the two peoples had become one nation, united by the laws which both accepted and by common loyalty to kings whom both acclaimed —the Danes because Cnut and his two successors were of their own blood, the English because these kings were kings of England, maintaining the old institutions and the ancient laws of the realm. But now this brief interlude of foreign rule was over. The house of Cerdic was once again at the head of Wessex and of England. Through intermarriage the royal families of Wessex and Mercia had come together in the past, so that in Edward's veins flowed not only the blood of Cerdic but the blood of Offa the near-legendary King of the Angles. Edward, descendant of Alfred under whom England had so mightily prospered, and in whose person all the bygone kings of Wessex were embodied, was home. The sceptre of England was again held by its rightful owner and the hearts of all men must have stirred with hope of a renewal of old felicities and of old glories.

IX

DANISH LAW AND LANGUAGE

THE invasion of England by the Danes and Scandinavians had been no less persistent than the invasion of Britain by the Angles and Saxons. It had continued for two centuries and had probably brought as many people, or indeed, more, into the island. Many of them had come from the same lands as their Anglo-Saxon predecessors, for Denmark is the modern name for the Cimbric peninsula which Ptolemy the Geographer had noted as the home of the Saxons in the second century. Others had come from Norway and the lands of the Baltic sea. But all shared, both with one another and with the Anglo-Saxons, many common traditions and customs and all spoke related languages. For a time the new intruders were a totally hostile people, but they were never totally alien. Their destinies were presided over by the same deities: the English had worshipped Woden; the new folk knew the All-Father as Odin. Both knew Thor the god of thunder and many other of the gods of the north.

Both were military societies, the essential unit being a chief and his companions, bound together by loyalty and a defiance of danger. Among the Angles and Saxons a chief's immediate followers and bodyguard were known as his *heorth-werode*, his 'hearth-troop'. These men did not merely follow their chief in war, but dwelt with him in his hall, and sat round his own hearth, bound by ties of personal friendship as well as by traditional loyalty. Among the new people, the war-leaders had a similar group of close companions, his *hus-carles* or 'house-troop'. The word *carl* was very close to the Saxon word *ceorl*, a free man. (It is, by the way, a comment upon changing standards that the word *ceorl* or churl has so sadly declined. The townsmen of later ages found the independent free farmer was taciturn to the point of gruffness, and lacking in the finer points of manners. To be churlish is no more a matter of pride.)

Just as the Anglo-Saxon people had brought into England their ancient institution of the assembly, adapting it to suit the pattern of the wider kingdoms they created in the island, so the Danes and Scandinavians brought with them the traditions of meetings (which they called *Things*) where matters affecting a whole group were discussed and in which laws were framed and enforced. So the two people shared the tradition of government by consultation and of the reinforcement of loyalty by close collaboration between leader and led.

At the time of the invasions the traditions of the two people were not identical. Three centuries and more had passed since the Angles and Saxons had left their European homelands to seek a new land in the island of Britain. During those centuries there had been many changes wrought among them, and different changes among their kinsfolk and their one-time neighbours on the continent. But the customs, institutions and languages of the new settlers still had much in common with those of the English, and the two peoples were able to merge more swiftly and completely than the mere tale of battle and bloodshed might suggest. Both, moreover, had come to the island by sea. Both knew, and had implanted in them as part of their heritage, the sound of the wind in the rigging, the thunder of the waves breaking on steep cliff and jagged rocks, the bitter sting of snow sweeping horizontally across the black waters of a wintry ocean, and the hard work at oar-bench, with shoulders aching and hearts envious of gannet and gull riding without effort on the cold wind.

Though by now the English were no more sea-raiders, their

memory of the sea and its ways was still fresh and still the subject of many of their songs. They would have found more in common with the tall pirates from the north, whose ships' companies were harrying their land from Cornwall to Northumbria, than with the dark Britons, many of whom lived peaceably in the English lands but whose own kingdoms still smouldered with unquenched hostility along their borders. The Anglo-Saxon people had absorbed many of the older British population, had framed special laws to deal with them, had often fought with them, and had sometimes made allies of them. But it was to be expected that the absorption of the Danes and Scandinavians, because of the similarity of institutions and language, would be swifter and more complete. Within modern Britain the separate identity and language of at least part of the Britons lives on in Wales. But the identity of the Danes is totally lost. Nowhere in England is their language spoken, and nowhere can any group be clearly seen as Danish. The merging of the two peoples was total. And because it was total, the size and importance of the Scandinavian and Danish element in the Anglo-Saxon people is sometimes overlooked.

Although the first Danes landed in the south at Portland, and although later fleets raided the Channel coast from Sandwich to Cornwall, it was along the eastern seaboard that the great weight of the raids was felt and where the first pirate-settlers turned from robbery to farming, setting up their permanent homes. They were deep-sea sailors who from the start felt no need merely to hug the coast of Europe and then to strike across the narrow seas to Kent or Wessex as the Angles and Saxons had first done. The wide North Sea was merely their pathway. They made landfall all along the east of England, in Kent, in East Anglia, in Lindsey, in Yorkshire and in Northumbria, and they came in vast numbers. The *Anglo-Saxon Chronicle*, recording the traditions of the coming of the first English, tells of leaders arriving with three ships or with five. During the Scandinavian invasion it tells of many fleets of more than a hundred sail, and of some larger still. The new invaders landed whole armies and the *Chronicle* always refers to them as *the her*, the host. When the first host wintered in England and when later the first settlers took farms in the island, many hundreds and possibly many thousands of men were involved.

It is therefore along the eastern coast of England, and in particular in the north, that traces of this massive settlement are mostly to be found. When Alfred agreed with Guthrun upon the boundaries that would divide the lands of the Danish settlements from the rest of the kingdom, it was laid down in the treaty that the frontier should run 'up the Thames, then up the Lea and along the Lea to its source. Then straight to Bedford, then up the Ouse to Watling Street'. This arrangement recognised a state of affairs that already existed. Alfred was not ceding fresh territory to the Danes—indeed, he had driven them out of parts of Wessex into which they had intruded. The treaty recorded the frontier of the lands where they had already settled in large numbers and in which Alfred undertook to leave them in peace. Through all the later conflicts and the changing fortunes of war, Alfred's successors substantially maintained the same boundaries. Within their area, which came to be known as the Danelaw, the Danes lived on, and Danish law persisted. Later, under their own kings, the Danes took lands west of Watling Street and south of the Thames. But the bulk of the settlements took place behind their original frontier; and it is in the lands of Guthrun that today there are the thickest clusters of Scandinavian and Danish place names.

The Danish word for a village was, and still is, *by*. Along the eastern half of England the word survives in the names of numerous towns and villages large and small : Whitby, Grimsby, Saxby and Kirby, attest the presence of the Danes in the east of England, and the building of new settlements or the renaming of old ones. Many of these places also embody the names of the settlers who first established them; Professor Stenton in his book *Anglo-Saxon England* instances Braceby, Rauceby, Laceby and Winceby, which contain the names of Breithr, Rauthr, Leifr and Vindr. The Danes used another word, *thorp*, for a small village or hamlet. This too survived in numerous towns and villages in the Danelaw. Mablethorpe, Trusthorpe and Theddlesthorpe tell of the longships landing on the coasts of Lincolnshire, and of the making of their settlements. Southwards lie Authorpe Row, Addlesthorpe and Winthorp. Between the coast and the city of Lincoln are numerous *by* names—Bilsby, Ketsby, Enderby, Wickenby and many others. The *thorps* and *bys* spread westwards from Lincoln and south-westwards along the Fosse Way, the old Roman road down which the Danish host must have ridden. Northwards are Cleethorpes and Scunthorpe in Lincolnshire. The Danish settlements in Yorkshire are commemorated in Nunthorp, Waverthorpe, Tibthorpe and similar names, and in the numerous *by* names such as Wetherby, Thornaby, Kirkby, Ainderby and Selby.

Other place names which tell of Scandinavian settlements are those ending in beck (a stream), fell (Danish *fjeld* and Norse *fiall*, a field), force (*fors*, a waterfall), gill (Norse *gil* or *geil* a narrow valley), how (Norse *haug-r* a mound) thwaite (Norse for a piece of land), wick (*vik* a village) and, with (Norse *vith-r* and Danish *ved* a wood). A glance at a map of eastern England will find many examples.

Altogether it has been estimated that there are some 1400 place names of Scandinavian origin in England. Over 400 (nearly one-third) are in Yorkshire, some 300 in Linconshire, 90 in Leicestershire, and about 100 divided between Norfolk and Northamptonshire. Clearly, in the Danelaw the number of Scandinavian settlers was extremely high and if the ethnic proportion bears any relation—as it probably does—to the proportion of these place names, then the blood of the Danes and Norsemen still flows abundantly in the veins of the Anglo-Saxon people, particularly in those from the east and north-east of England. But Scandinavians also settled beyond their formal frontiers. In Cumberland and Westmorland there are are 150 significant place names and in Lancashire over 50. The rest are scattered widely over the country, evidence of the peaceful settlement of Danish and Norse folk in Mercia and Wessex.

In spite of all the proofs (to be found both in the place-names and in the *Anglo-Saxon Chronicle*'s references to vast fleets) of the enormous numbers of Scandinavian people settled in the island, there was probably no large-scale substitution of a Scandinavian population for an English one. Wholesale looting there certainly was in the early days, with much slaughter of the English both on the battlefield and in monastery and homestead. But at the time of the major settlements the island was by no means crowded; good land was still to be won from the waste and good farms to be had by clearing moorland and forest. In the north certainly the Danish settlements appear to have been made in new lands rather than by the dispossession of the English farmers. The cases of siege and capture, of farms left empty because their English owner had fallen in battle against victorious sea-rovers, were probably few in relation to the numbers of Danes and Norsemen who cut back the forests, cleared the waste land and set the bright emerald of new pasture and new corn in the broad lands of golden bracken and silver birch woods.

Intermarriage between the old people and the new must have started fairly early. The Danes came as an army, and on the long and dangerous voyage over the North Sea, with battle and long marches awaiting them, it is inconceivable that they should have brought their own womenfolk. We know from the records that, in the days of their early raids the prizes they took included slaves whom they sold on the continent. Some of these they would have kept, and perhaps the first Anglo-Danish household was built around an arrogant conqueror and his sullen and unwilling women. But this process could not for long have met the needs of the growing Scandinavian population. Far more likely is the gradual acceptance by both folk that the Danes and the Norsemen now formed part of the local population and that marriages between the two people were to be taken for granted. The early Christianisation of the Danes would have hastened the intermingling. (At least one English surname commemorates this process for the name Haldane was once Half-Dane.) Later, when the Danes firmly held the east of England and when, in the days of Aethelred, English resistance proved ineffective and unlucky, some Danes would have felt sufficiently secure to bring over their wives and sisters, but the vast majority of those who lived in England, as farmers or townsmen, must inevitably have taken local wives. And the local population was frequently, as we have seen, of mixed descent. In Yorkshire, where the Scandinavian newcomers settled very early, and where Scandinavian kings like Eric Bloodaxe had ruled independently in the city of York, the blood of the Britons no doubt still flowed in the veins of the local English. For we have seen how York had been at least once the centre of British resistance and had been for a while the royal city of a British king.

So to a people descended from Celtic Britons, from soldiers and settlers of the Roman period, and from Angles and Saxons, was added the Danish and Scandinavian element. And although the assimilation of the new folk was complete, and their language vanished together with their separate identity, the Anglo-Saxon people of England were greatly modified in the process. Their language, law, institutions and character took on, and still retain, new qualities and characteristics.

The language of the Danes was closely allied to that of the English. When, at the battle of Maldon, the spokesman of the Danes called across the dividing river to Byrhtnoth and his followers, the poem mentions no interpreter; the two armies understood one another's demands and defiances. Milk and bread, sword and fight, son and daughter, field and house, cow and bull—the basic words were common to both people. Once the Danelaw was permanently inhabited by the new people from the north, a common language of necessity had to be developed from the common basis. Because of the massive Scandinavian population and because of the political power of the newcomers in the Danelaw, that language might well have been Norse or Danish, with the conquered English unwillingly learning the speech of their new and dominant neighbours. But the English language is strangely powerful and persistent. It remained for example in the Lowlands of Scotland long after all the other effects of Northumbria's invasions had been forgotten. It was adopted by all the Britons who lived on in the English kingdoms, and even by those living in the disputed border country. In modern times it has shown the same power of intrusion and survival. Throughout England including the Danelaw its triumph was total. When Cnut, the Danish King of England, issued letters to his people, these letters were in English.

The English language made many borrowings from the speech of the new people, however, and enriched itself in the process. Many of the borrowed words tell something of the kind of people the Danes were and how they were seen by the English : to ransack is a Norse word! When the Danes' *thing* or assembly sat or was selected at the house of the king or leader it was called the *hus-thing*, and the hustings are with us today. The word 'law' is also Scandinavian, for the English spoke of *dooms*. The new people were less barbaric than the tale of their harryings would suggest; they shared with the English a respect for a written set of rules designed to give stability to society. In fact the Danes had in their courts twelve 'lawmen' who were under oath to make good and honest judgment in the cases put before them, and some have seen in this the origins of the English jury system. This may be fanciful, for juries as such were not known until after the Normans came. What is certain, however, is that the Danes and the Norsemen relied upon law as much as the English did, and that they caused no break in the continuity of English law. Cnut was a great lawgiver, continuing the work of his Saxon predecessors. By-laws, of course, are the special local laws laid down for a *by* or town.

The Scandinavian languages tended to have *sk* or *sc* where English had *sh*. 'Skirt' and 'scrub' were added to the native 'shirt' and 'shrub'. 'Scab' also came from the Norse, as did 'scar' for a steep mountainside, 'scare' and 'scold'. Nor did the newcomers live only within the towns and boroughs; the word 'ploughland' is theirs, and 'skin' and 'skiver' show Norsemen at work on country crafts. Such everyday words suggest a close relationship between the two people, in the towns and courts, in farm and village, in the countryside, at work and at home.

The Danes and Norsemen of course brought much else to alter the character of the English scene. One of the main differences between the Danish invaders and the first waves of the Angles and Saxons in earlier days was that the latter had first settled along the coasts and did not at once penetrate deeply into the countryside. Moreover they did not swiftly take the ruined Roman cities nor make them their first centres. In many instances they built their own towns somewhat apart from them, as if they found the great buildings and paved streets oppressive. The massive Danish armies, on the other hand, very soon after their first coastal raids, swept over the country and were quick to seize many cities, making the bases first of their raids and later of their settled territories. The *Anglo-Saxon Chronicle* mentions hosts centred upon Cambridge, upon London and upon the five boroughs in the north. York became the centre of an independent Scandinavian kingdom. The new folk very swiftly became town dwellers and burgesses. Because the Danes were so successful in their use of fortified towns, King Alfred and the later kings of Wessex renovated city fortifications and built new boroughs. Both within and without the Danelaw, town life began to flourish, taking on an importance and influence which it had previously lacked.

Next, there is no evidence that the Angles and Saxons maintained any significant contact with their original homelands, nor with the other tribes which had migrated elsewhere. They were content for their lives to be bounded by the seas that beat upon the shores of England, by the Wall to the north and the mountains of the west. Within a generation or two they had become islanders, maintaining some contact with Rome, as good and devout Christians, and with the near kingdoms of the Franks. The Danes and Norsemen on the other hand were in continuous contact with their kinsmen oversea. From the Danish settlement round Dublin they invited a king to rule over them in the north, and of the Danes who fought at Brunnanburgh many had sailed from the mouth of the Liffey. Under Cnut, England formed part of a great Scandinavian empire, for Norway, Denmark and Sweden all owed allegiance to the same king who governed England. Events on the Continent, a naval battle in the Baltic, the alliances and policies of Continental rulers, all these began to have an importance for England, and England began to grow aware of them. The Anglo-Saxon people, having paused for a century or two within its new island, was beginning once more to look outwards beyond its own misty horizon.

The wars between the invading Danes and the English, as well as the coming to power of a Danish king over the whole people, forced England into a unity that otherwise might have been long delayed. The English people, coming to a land that had once, south of the Wall, been a single Roman province, bound together by roads and defended towns, had begun very early to see their new country as a single unit, ruled over by one man. We have seen how early some English kings took the title of *Bretwalda*. But it was on the anvil of battle with the Danes that real nationhood was hammered out. The stubborn resistance of Wessex under Alfred, when all the other kingdoms had fallen, gave a new hope to all Englishmen—Northumbrians, Mercians, East Anglians and West Saxons alike; and the Kings of Wessex became evidently and surely the Kings of England. The common subjection to Danish kings for a brief while reinforced the strength of the new-found unity and gave to the Scandinavian folk a sense of identity with the older people. By a paradox that is not hard to understand, it was under Danish kings that the Danes finally became part of the Anglo-Saxon people.

The old separate kingdoms became administrative political units within the realm of England. Under the Saxon kings, a man who held great power under the crown and who exercised some part of the royal authority was called on *ealdorman*, an alderman. The title is akin to that of the Roman senator, a senior or elder chosen from the people to assist the king. Next to the king's own title, it is the oldest in England. Many great men had held it and had given it new lustre: Byrhtnoth, the hero of Maldon, whose bravery shines against the darkness of the rest of King Aethelred's reign, was an alderman. When the kings of Wessex became kings of England they set up aldermen to be their deputies in their wider kingdoms. But the Danish and Norse war-leaders, under the king, had the title of *jarl*, which on English tongues became earl, and this for the most part replaced the name of alderman. The deputy of the King of England in the old kingdom of Wessex became an Earl of Wessex and similar dignitaries were placed in the other ancient kingdoms. The gentle earls who today sit in the House of Lords are the inheritors of a dignity first borne by tall sea-rovers; while the quiet and earnest aldermen who sit on English city councils bear an even older title that once was earned at the sword's edge.

The pressure of the Danish invasions, and later the rule of Danish kings, brought about another important innovation. The Saxon system of taxation had been elementary and inefficient. The kings depended for their wealth upon their personal estates and upon the *feorm*, the taxes paid in kind by the landowners, which as already noted provided for the upkeep of the royal household and of the principal officers. In the absence of any regular money revenue it was difficult for a strong central government to develop. But when Aethelred tried to buy off the Danes, they had to be paid in gold and silver. The king's subjects had to be taxed in terms of money, the Danegeld, and an organisation for this purpose had to be built. Aethelstan had earlier employed clerks and secretaries to strengthen and communicate his authority so that the crude foundations of a civil service had been laid. Later, Cnut imposed further taxes when he became King of England: a tax to pay the crews of his ships, and a tax to pay his housecarls. The people became accustomed to pay for the king's protection and government, and the kings began to develop an organisation through which taxes could be assessed and collected. This too was an influence towards unity, and upon it later kings were to build an imposing and enduring structure.

One institution the Danes shattered for a while. In the days of their early raiding they savagely attacked the monasteries of northern England; monks were slaughtered, libraries burned, and treasure looted. The tradition of learning and scholarship was for a while destroyed, and in the north the monasteries never fully recovered from those terrible days. In the south however, under the strong shield of Wessex, learning was rekindled and monks could flourish.

By the early tenth century, the Anglo-Saxon people were again a single and united nation, having absorbed the incomers of the eighth and ninth centuries and having enriched their language, their institutions and their character by so doing. They were now about to receive the last of the great invasions and, once more, were to absorb and transform the invaders.

X

THE COMING OF THE NORMANS

THE Danes and Scandinavians who harried England were not the only adventurers to set sail from the northern fjords and havens in search of new adventures and new kingdoms. Some had gone to Ireland, seizing Dublin and the land round about. Some took their dragon-prowed ships through the cold and mountainous seas of the North Atlantic, to the Orkneys and to Greenland. Leif Ericsson journeyed westwards to Vinland, which may have been America, anticipating Columbus by many centuries. Others took their armies to the rich lands south of the English Channel and plundered the kingdom of the Franks—the one-time prosperous Roman province of Gaul. In Alfred's day the *Anglo-Saxon Chronicle* was already recording battles between the Franks and the pirate host. In AD 883 'the host went up the Somme to Amiens and remained there for one year'. Two years later the host marched westwards and spent the winter on the river Seine. In the following year they went through Paris and along the Seine to the Marne. By AD 890 there was fighting as far to the west as Brittany. Twenty-five years afterwards 'a big army sailed over hither from the south from Brittany under two jarls Ohtor and Hroald and sailed west about until they reached the river Severn'.

Among the host of Northmen invading France at this time was an army led by an ambitious warrior named Rollo. He seized the town of Rouen on the river Seine, much as the Danes in England were occupying towns and boroughs and basing their armies upon them. The King of France, Charles the Simple, made peace with Rollo in AD 911 and Rollo was granted the city of Rouen and much of the land round about. He became a Christian and though he held his new territory as a subordinate of the King of France, he was virtually an independent ruler, with the title of Duke. To Rollo's territory a new name was given. The French knew the host by the Norsemen's own name for themselves—Northmen. But on French tongues the word became 'Norman' and the land became known as Normandy.

In AD 1002 came Aethelred of England's second marriage, to Emma, sister of Richard, duke of Normandy, the descendant of Rollo. Because of this union, Aethelred was able to seek refuge in Normandy after the Danish victories in England, and as already seen it was in Normandy that his son Edward remained during the period of the Danish kings. Edward was thus closely linked to the Normans, not only by ties of blood but by gratitude. By the time he came to the throne of England, the Dukedom of Normandy was held by a young man named William, the illegitimate son of the former Duke, Robert the Devil. Through Emma, William was Edward's cousin and the two men had much in common. Edward had come to the throne of England after years of exile when he must have had little hope of ever achieving the kingdom to which his descent entitled him. William too had inherited his title in times of turmoil, while still a child, and for long years of struggle and civil war his authority was in doubt. Though he was his father's acknowledged heir, there were many who rejected the idea that a bastard son of a mere tanner's daughter could ever be Duke of Normandy.

When aged twenty-four and secure in his dukedom, he crossed the Channel in state and visited his cousin King Edward of England. The two would have had much to discuss, of past dangers and present power, and many memories to share. Years afterwards William claimed that during these conversations Edward had privately made him heir to the crown of England. If so, Edward had carried friendship and gratitude beyond the bounds of legality. True, William was Edward's cousin, but only through Emma, and William himself was not a member of the royal house of England. Moreover the crown of England was not a property that a king could bestow upon a selected heir. It was the Witan which selected or confirmed a new monarch. However the prospect of exchanging a ducal coronet for a kingly crown was apparently a glittering one, and possible enough for William to pursue relentlessly over the years. Diplomatically, he recognised the immense importance of a link with the house of Cerdic which, but for the brief interlude of the Danish dynasty, had furnished the kings of Wessex and then of England for six hundred years, and he married Matilda, a descendant through the female line of Alfred, whose memory still dominated men's minds in England, and whose laws were still a symbol of English freedom and English independence.

Meantime Edward ruled in England, but the high hopes with which his reign had begun soon faded. His years as an exile had separated him from the traditions and customs of the realm. He left much of the task of government to others, devoting himself more and more to religious matters; Westminster Abbey, which he caused to be built and where he still lies buried, is his chief memorial. But the sterner work of kingship was given to others, among them Godwin, Earl of Wessex. Edward married Godwin's daughter and Godwin became almost as powerful as the king himself.

Then, in the same year that William visited the king, there was an affray at Dover between a party of Frenchmen, under Eustace, husband of King Edward's sister, and the townsmen. Twenty Englishmen were killed and nineteen Frenchmen. Edward was furious, summoned Godwin, and insisted that he should march against Dover. Godwin refused to make war against his own people and raised an army against the king. As a result Godwin and his two sons, Harold and Swegen, were banished. But they were later restored, their influence more firmly established than ever. When Godwin died, Harold succeeded him. Brother-in-law of the king, Earl of the old kingdom

K

of Wessex and therefore inheritor of some of its glory, a tried soldier and a champion of the English cause against the French friends and kinsmen of the king, Harold was the greatest man in England under the crown. It was his prowess and not King Edward's that led English armies to victory. In AD 1056, for example, an English host rode against Griffin, the Welsh king. The English were led by a militant bishop who was slain in the fighting. 'It is hard to tell' says the *Chronicle*, 'the wretchedness and the marching and the fighting, and all the labour and the loss of men and of horses too which the English host suffered' until Earl Leofric and Earl Harold came to their rescue. It was the hands of Harold that now wielded the sword of Wessex, while the hands of King Edward were clasped in prayer.

If William was to inherit the crown of England, it was not enough for him to claim King Edward as his cousin, nor to have the king's promise. It was not even enough for him to have taken a descendant of Alfred to wife and so to have united himself with the house and blood of the legendary Cerdic. He would require the support, willingly given if possible, of Harold the acknowledged ruler of Wessex and the unacknowledged but effective ruler of England. Some years before Harold's rescue of the English army from the victorious and revengeful Welsh, William by chance was given the opportunity that he needed. Harold was shipwrecked in the Channel and came ashore on the Normandy coast. William kept him at his court, some said as a welcome guest and some said as a prisoner, and during this time Harold swore an oath to support William's claim to be the heir of Edward. Harold claimed afterwards that his oath had been obtained by duress or trickery and might therefore, in accordance with the laws of Alfred, be considered void.

A few years later, all these matters moved to their climax. The great Abbey church, which Edward had built by the Thames west of London, was completed. At Christmas the king visited it and on 28 December 1065 it was consecrated. Eight days later, his life's work completed, Edward died. The writer of the *Chronicle*, in a stilted poem in his praise, recalled his days of exile and the long years when England was ruled by Danish kings. But of Edward himself he could find little to say except the conventional and traditional phrases. Harold, Earl of Wessex, was consecrated king in his place. For the first time for six centuries (apart from the interlude of the Danish kings) Wessex and England had a king who was not descended from Cerdic. Under him, in spite of his prowess and courage, the nation was to suffer swift defeat and long humiliation.

In Normandy, Duke William was making preparations to press his claim to the crown by force of arms. His army was drawn not only from his own land of Normandy but from Flanders, Brittany, and other parts of France, and a massive fleet was built to transport it to England. By the late summer all his preparations were complete. Ships and men were poised for the invasion of England.

Throughout the long summer days, Harold's ships patrolled the Channel and his army, consisting of farmers and cottagers from all the shires of England, was stationed along the coast ready to beat off any attack. The men had been under arms all summer, provisions were running out and the harvest stood golden in their distant fields, ready to be gathered. At the end of the first week of September 1066 they were therefore disbanded and allowed to go home. The ships sailed round the coast of Kent, up the Thames estuary and were moored off London.

Immediately afterwards, and just when England's defences had been dismantled in this way, news came of an invasion in the north. King Harald of Norway, supported by Tostig the exiled brother of Harold of England, had landed with a great host, ostensibly to win an earldom for Tostig but in fact to make a bid for the realm. The Norwegian host moved on York, once the stronghold of an independent Norse kingdom and still the centre of a largely Scandinavian population. Harold of England hastened north by forced marches with such troops as were still available. Together with the Earls Edwin and Morcar, two brothers who ruled the north, Harold's men fought two pitched battles against the Norwegian host in five desperate days and

were in the end victorious. The final battle at Stamford Bridge
was hard fought; many of the English were slain, more were
wounded and all were weary. But there was no time for either
respite or rest. The battle of Stamford Bridge was fought on
Monday 25 September. On the morning of Thursday in
the same week, the fleet of William of Normandy came to
anchor at Pevensey, and William's army came ashore unopposed.

When the news reached Harold, he marched his weary army

THE NORMANS DISEMBARK THEIR HORSES AT PEVENSEY
(FROM THE BAYEUX TAPESTRY)

south again. There was no time to recall the men who had been
sent back to their waiting farms two fatal weeks earlier. Nor
could Edwin and Morcar spare any troops from the north, for
the Norwegian army, though defeated, was not destroyed and
its ships still lay menacingly in the northern English havens. So
with his own housecarls and those of his two brothers, about
seven thousand men all told, many of them battle-weary and
exhausted by their swift marches to York and back, Harold
moved south to face William's army, which was by now rested
from the sea-journey and was awaiting the trial of battle with
joyful confidence.

The English took up a defensive position on high ground
near Hastings, by a pool called in their own language Sandlake,
and which later French chroniclers referred to as Senlac. The

Norman army moved to the attack and first blood was drawn by the English. For a while they were successful, standing firm behind their shield-wall and beating back charge after charge of the Norman armoured cavalry. Many men fell, and among them King Harold's two brothers. Then, patience lost and desperately eager to make an end of the long fighting, some of the English left the safety of the shield-wall to pursue a body of Norman horsemen who had fallen back from the terrible battle-axes of the housecarls. Suddenly the horsemen rallied, exhorted by Duke William himself, swung their horses swiftly, and turned on their English pursuers. The latter, caught off balance and far from the safety of their own lines, were cut down by the Norman swords. William was quick to learn the lesson. From time to time, bodies of Norman horsemen would attack the stubborn shield-wall, turn away and canter back as if in terrified retreat, tempting more and more of the English host to pursue them with the same fatal outcome. Harold himself died, killed by a volley of arrows shot at random into the English position. As at Maldon, where Bryhtnoth's companions and thanes were proudly resolved to die with their slaughtered lord, so now did Harold's housecarls form a circle round the king's lifeless body and grimly wield their battle-axes while the light of day endured, their circle growing smaller but no less firm and no less stubborn. One by one they died, axe in hand, and by nightfall William was master of the desolate field of Sandlake and the whole realm of England lay ready to be taken.

Harold's body was taken to Waltham Abbey, north-east of London, while William turned eastwards into Kent and secured the vital port of Dover. English resistance centred on Prince Edgar, known as Edgar Aetheling, a direct descendant of Cerdic and of Alfred. The citizens of London proclaimed him king and looked to their defences. At first, hope and defiance were strong enough: during the long period of the Danish wars England had been invaded and English armies defeated. There was noth-ing in the present situation to cause despair. A new army might be raised and the Norman host driven back over the sea. Edgar enjoyed a brief period of hope and glory as King of England, safe in the walled city of London.

Then William moved north to the attack and attempted to force London Bridge. His advance guard was beaten back by Edgar's men. William, in what must have seemed to the victorious Londoners a useless act of vengeful despair, burnt Southwark to the ground and moved westwards away from the embattled city. He crossed the Thames at Wallingford and went northwards to Berkhampstead. Quite suddenly the resistance of the English collapsed and at Berkhampstead their leaders, including Edgar himself, Edwin and Morcar, the Archbishop of Canterbury and the leading citizens of London, made submission to William and took oaths of loyalty to him. By force of arms he had made good his claim to be Edward's heir and, some three months after landing, he was crowned King of England on Christmas Day in the new Abbey of Westminster so recently completed by Edward.

Within six months William felt sufficiently secure to leave the island and to visit Normandy. In the winter he returned to his new kingdom, twelve months after his coronation. Discontent was smouldering among the English and news came that Exeter had declared its defiance of the new king, William marched westwards with a combined force of English and Norman troops. Then the North rose against him. Edgar, realising that the spirit of resistance was still alive in England, repented of his submission, fled from William's court and took refuge with King Malcolm of Scotland. Edwin and Morcar too defected and returned to their earldom in the north. York became the centre of a new English resistance, and William had once more to fight for possession of his new kingdom. He was again successful and the northern English made submission to him.

But in the following year there were more risings, and a Norman army was destroyed in Durham. Then, dramatically, King Swein of Denmark sent over a fleet of nearly two hundred and fifty ships to make a bid for the crown of England. He was Cnut's heir; and English and Dane had lived together long enough for the people of England to see the Danish army not as invaders but as deliverers. Swein's fleet made a show of force at Dover and Sandwich and then sailed north to safe anchorage in the Humber. Meantime in Yorkshire a fresh English army had been raised by Edgar Aetheling and other English leaders. The Anglo-Danish army marched upon York and drove out the Normans, slaughtering the garrison.

As the news of the coming of the Danish host spread throughout England, hope and resolution alike revived in the hearts of the people and there was widespread fighting. Wessex and Mercia rose against William, and the Normans were hard-pressed. Heartened by all that he heard of William's peril, King Swein himself sailed from Denmark and joined his fleet, still lying at anchor in the Humber. The Danish host set up their stronghold at Ely where many Englishmen flocked to join them. Most prominent among them was Hereward, a thane who lived in Lincolnshire and who resisted the Normans doggedly. With resolute singleness of purpose, he treated as friends all men, whether of English or of Danish descent, who opposed the Normans, and as enemies all who supported the invaders or fell under their power. Although originally a protector of the English monastery of Peterborough, when he heard that William had appointed a French abbot, Turold, he and his men stormed the building, set it on fire, and seized its treasure, even to the gold crown from the head of Christ on the great crucifix. Outlawed by the Norman authorities, feared by all for his ruthlessness, Hereward the Wake lived on in legend as a fierce symbol of Anglo-Saxon resistance.

Then in the summer of AD 1070 William and Swein made peace and the King of Denmark agreed to remove his fleet from the Humber and his men from Ely. Hereward continued the war almost single-handed. For nearly a year he held out in the Fens, joined from time to time by other warlike and stubborn Englishmen. Finally, he and his men cut their way out of the Isle of Ely and William's task of conquest was completed.

He had taken the realm of England, as a prize won in the

tumult and desolation of many battles. English, Danish and Norman blood had stained the trampled earth of hillside and field, from Sussex to Yorkshire and beyond. What he had taken by force, he held by terror. He built castles from which his garrisons could dominate the sullen and defeated English; he built the Tower of London, using as foundations a part of the now legendary Roman works which still stood there. Along the borders of Wales, in the lands which still lay in dispute between the independent Britons and the old kingdom of Mercia, he set up further castles to mark his authority and to daunt any attempts by the Britons to break into his kingdom. The great estates of England were given to the Norman and Breton land-owners who had brought their men into his army for the invasion. The burning of cities, the devastation of farms, and the destruction of the rich harvests in the fields—all these things were instruments which William used to punish insurrection and to discourage further rebellion.

And yet he did not see himself as a foreign king governing a hostile people who had become his unwilling subjects by mere conquest. He considered himself the heir of Edward and in his rightful place. He himself was the restorer of the ancient English kingdom : not only was he cousin to the dead King Edward, but he could also claim kinship with Cnut, the acknowledged king of England, while his wife was a princess of the house of Cerdic and Alfred. Harold had been a mere usurper.

As we have seen, the army with which he put down the rebellion at Exeter was made up of English and Norman alike. Until they finally turned against him, he received Edwin and Morcar as members of his council. Edgar, who had been pro-claimed king in London, and whom William might well have put to death as a most dangerous rival, was received as a guest at his court and was numbered among his advisers. It was Edgar who finally fled from William's court to make a bid for the crown of his ancestors, and not William who exiled him. William assured the citizens of London that he would respect their ancient and immemorial rights. He undertook to uphold the laws of Edward and maintained all the institutions and customs of the land. Some new laws he did introduce in order to protect the men from Normandy and France who had now settled in England as landowners; but for the most part the laws of the kingdom remained.

The Norman conquest was not like the English conquest six hundred years earlier: William's victories were swift, sudden and self-contained. There was no repetition of the migration of whole peoples, decade by decade and century by century, across the lonely seas to take land in the green island of Britain. Nor was it like the Danish invasions which continued over two centuries and more, and which planted Danes and Norwegians, year by year, throughout the whole land. There were no areas of the kingdom occupied by a new people, as Kent had been occupied by the English or Yorkshire by the Danes. Celt and Saxon, Angle and Dane, had made their clearings in the forest and built their farms and villages, giving them names in their own tongues which live on to this day. Not so the Normans; they were a small military aristocracy who built tall castles and took the great houses of their predecessors. The new blood came in but sparsely, and mainly at one level of society. The soldiers who came for the swift conquest of England were a mere hand-ful compared with the Anglo-Saxon and Danish invaders of earlier generations. Moreover, although the king and the new aristocracy were foreign, they were not completely alien. William's piratical ancestor, who had won his dukedom in savage battle against the French king, was close kin to those other Northmen who had harried England and set up their independent kingdoms there. Strangely, too, some of the old blood of Britain came back to the island with Duke William. For among his followers, and among those who were given land in England, were men from Brittany—descendants of those Britons who had crossed the Channel as refugees in the dark days when the English first came.

The Norman conquest did not, therefore, have far-reaching ethnic consequences. The Anglo-Saxon people, with its Celtic and Scandinavian mixture, was now governed by a foreign king and subjected to a foreign aristocracy; but though its experience was enlarged, its character was not greatly changed.

The social and political results were of course profound, permeating almost every aspect of the nation's life. The English

ROCHESTER CASTLE, BUILT BY THE NORMANS ON A
ROMAN SITE

imbibed a taste for foreign wars and were given possessions across the seas; more than once William led an English army to fight his wars in France. For the first time since their arrival in Britain, the English were at war on the Continent. They were soon to forget that technically it was Normandy that owned England, and for many centuries were to fight over and guard lands in France which they saw as their own.

At home, the most spectacular changes first affected the great families, the thanes and earls who were dispossessed, their lands handed to Norman barons. One by one the sees of England came to be held by Norman bishops. The king's authority was emphasised throughout the land, grimly symbolised by the menacing walls of the new castles. The tenant farmers were largely left with their farms, but under new and foreign lords, and with the simple rents they were accustomed to pay, of ale and corn, of barley and of work upon the lord's land, now supplemented by the rent of military service. French became the language of the king's representatives, of the courts, of government and of the aristocracy. Yet although no man could prosper or move among the great ones if he lacked French, the English language obstinately persisted, with undiminished vigour, in the farms, streets and cottages of the kingdom. For three long centuries and more it lived as a spoken rather than a written tongue. The old poetry and the old learning which had briefly blossomed in England seemed to die, but in fact it never withered entirely. The language (its vocabulary widened by centuries of contact with French, the forms of its poetry modified by the introduction of rhyme and by the formal syllabic count of French verse-forms, its prose retaining the muscular directness of pre-conquest days) re-emerged triumphantly after three hundred years and came to be used by king, aristocrat and peasant alike.

A chill wind of predetermined doom seems to blow through the oft-told tale of the Norman conquest. If only Harold had not had to face two invasions simultaneously, one by the Norwegians in the North and one by the Normans in the South; if only he had not marched to Hastings with a scant and weary army; if only Edgar Aetheling had been a more heroic and stalwart figure; if only the earls Edwin and Morcar had ridden southwards with their armies; if only the citizens of London had shown the same resolution as had their predecessors against the Danish invaders in earlier years; if only King Swein's men and Hereward's men had stood stoutly together in the Isle of Ely, making of it as unyielding a stronghold as Alfred had made of the Isle of Aethelney; if only all Wessex had risen in support of the citizens of Exeter; if only there had been an Englishman to unite all those separate forces which rebelled or fought against William—then the arms of England might have prevailed and the Norman invader might have been finally defeated.

Yet, because of the disasters to English arms, it was the fate of England to be drawn, through its Norman kings, into the affairs of Europe as Britain had been when she was the Roman Island, and to share intimately in the culture and life of Europe. The people remained. And the institutions, though modified by new rulers and with names altered, also remained. Descendants of Cerdic and of Alfred, through marriages with the new dynasty, remained and remain to this day on the throne of England. The meeting of the wise lost the name of Witan and was given the French name of *parlement*, but its traditions and power continued. The Norman conquest added something to the character, but did not break the continuity, of the story of the English people.

EPILOGUE

W ITHIN a few years of the Norman conquest, the Anglo-Saxon people had taken their final shape, bearing the indelible imprint of their origins and adventures, of their settling in a Romano-Celtic land, of their conflict with the Danes and finally with the Normans. In later ages other people were to come to the island, settle there, and mingle their blood with that of the English. Celts from Ireland, weavers and craftsmen from the Low countries, religious refugees from France, men from Scotland seeking their fortunes in the richer lands of the south—all these and many others over the centuries made their special contributions to the character and qualities of the people.

But the Norman conquest was the last of the great invasions and the last occasion upon which land was forcibly seized and some of the earlier inhabitants dispossessed. Now the English were to experience something of the sorrows they had imposed upon the Britons six hundred years before, when many, as Gildas tells us, crossed the seas 'with loud lamentations'. For at this time there is evidence of Englishmen serving in foreign armies. Some travelled as far as Constantinople to serve in the palace guard: no doubt these were sons of the once-rich families whose estates had passed into Norman hands. Moving through the marbled splendour of the Emperor's palace, looking out over the blue Bosphorous, these men knew that their timbered halls and green fields were now held by others and that their own lives were now to be lived across the lonely seas. They had undertaken wider adventures and longer journeys than those of their ancestors who had come to Britain, and had taken up again the roving destiny which for a while had been forgotten within the narrow confines of the island. But such emigrants were relatively few, and English and Norman settled down to live together.

During the five hundred years after the fall of the Roman Empire, when the tribes beyond Rome's frontier were breaking into the former provinces and there resuming their separate kingdoms, there was a degree of homogeneity among those nations who raided and settled in the one-time Roman island of Britain. The first Germanic invaders, the Angles, the Saxons and the Jutes, though differing in many ways had much in common. All spoke languages that each could understand; all worshipped the same gods, lived in the same kind of society, believed in the same kind of loyalties, and shared many common traditions. Whereas in other former Roman provinces the small barbarian kingdoms retained their separate identities almost into modern times, in Britain it became possible very early for the kings of Wessex to shape one single realm out of the diverse kingdoms. This ensured that the linguistic, institutional, sociological and military differences that had existed between the three peoples from Germany did not become divisive forces nor cause the development in isolation of fragmentary cultures. Each enriched the other within the framework of a unified England. Each made its contribution to the total character of the people.

It was not only the power of Wessex that made this unity possible. The new people were the political heirs of the old. The Britons who had opposed the first English invaders, though themselves divided, conceived Britain as a single political unit, remembering the days of Roman rule and the central authority which once held sway. The long and stubborn defence made by the Britons under such leaders as Ambrosius and Arthur gave time for the two peoples to learn about one another, and to share to some extent in one another's traditions. The resistance of the Britons lasted for many centuries, during which they passed on to the English the conception of one territorial and political unit, stretching from Hadrian's Wall to the high cliffs of the Channel. For this was the province over which the Romans had ruled and over which usurping Emperors in the island (who had become immortal figures in the legends and poems of the Britons) had once reigned as Lords of Britain. No doubt it was knowledge of these past events that prompted kings in England to assume the title of *Bretwalda* long before any unity had in fact been achieved. The example of history, magnified by the uncertain light and mists of legend, gave the English kings early aspirations towards unity and offered them a pattern to which to work.

England's good fortune continued during the troubled years of the Danish incursions. For the Danes too, as well as their associates from Norway and Sweden, were not wholly alien to the English people. Their language was similar as was their form of society. And although for a while they tried to carve out separate kingdoms, they inevitably came under the influence of the unity that had already developed. They soon adopted the language of the English and were content to be fellow-subjects of the English crown, whether the latter was borne by Englishman or Dane. They, too, became not a divisive but an enriching force in the formation of the Anglo-Saxon people. Their contribution was as important as it has been enduring. They brought the towns to life, deepened the conception of the law and added a new dimension to the national character.

By the time the Normans came the realm and people of England were so solidly built that there was no catastrophic change or dramatic discontinuity. The Northmen who had settled in Normandy had adopted French as their language, just as their kinfolk in England had adopted English, but after a few generations their descendants in England adopted the English tongue, to which a new depth had been given by long contact with the French language.

So England became a land where the northern tribes of Europe, or their most adventurous elements, could meet together and through conflict and rivalry develop a way of life that drew something from each. And this was done in a country where Roman roads and cities had survived, and where a Romano-Celtic population also made its contribution to the final result.

The most famous monument of King William's reign, Domesday Book, was compiled following the decision of the king's council at Gloucester in 1085 to make a complete survey of the kingdom, 'how it was peopled and with what kind of men'. The names of the owners and tenants of estates and farms in every county show something of the diverse origins of the English at this time. The evidence must be used with caution, for only those who paid taxes were listed, the great landlords and the tenant farmers; the cottagers and labourers remain anonymous. Moreover names do not tell everything of a man's descent. Domesday Book was made some six hundred years after the first coming of the English. In eighteen or twenty generations many of the Celtic families would have lost their individual identities and their names would mostly have vanished. Nevertheless, Domesday Book lists about thirty Celtic names among the landowners of England. There are other names of doubtful origin but which are probably British, giving a total of some fifty in all.

Of Danish names there are nearly ten times as many—about four hundred and fifty. They are thickest in Yorkshire, Lincolnshire and East Anglia, but are to be found throughout the kingdom. There are also some two hundred and fifty names of Frankish and Frisian origin, probably representing descendants of soldiers and captives brought from the Continent into England by the Danish armies.

No doubt among the unpropertied classes about whom Domesday Book is silent the situation would have been different. A smaller proportion of Danes would be likely, for the Danes were recent conquerors and their descendants would probably have been among the men of property. The number of men descended from the Britons might on the other hand have been higher, since they were the survivors of a conquered race.

All the invading peoples had of course been seafarers. Even the Normans were descended from men who had sailed westwards from their old homeland and up the estuary of the Seine. Once the Roman garrisons had left the island it had been open to any who were willing to trace their way through the sea, defy its dangers and take the risk of building new homes in a far land. Those tribes in Europe who moved westwards and southwards through vineyards and rich fields to win land and power had taken the deserted highways of the old Empire. The ships that came to Pegwell Bay and the many thousands that followed, turned their backs upon the turmoil of Europe to build a new country that was safe from all but seamen like themselves.

For a while all these people were too busy with the shaping of their new homes to leave their island and take to the sea again. But with England's destiny linked with the Continent by the Norman conquest, the descendants of the first English soldiers and of the seamen of the Danish fleet began to look outward again. Five hundred years later the English people were to repeat their adventures on other journeys, taking their tiny ships into all the seas of the world whether on war or on peaceful pilgrimage. From Devon and the west country, where there was probably the largest survival of British stock, they crossed the wide Atlantic. English ships were to travel to the most distant lands of the East, to the new world that lay beyond the sunset, to the green coasts of Africa and to new lands that they discovered to the south of Asia. In many of these lands they set up their homes, clearing the forests and planting their farms and orchards.

The journey from the pine-woods and sand-dunes of Germany, upon which Hengist's ships had embarked, was to last for one and a half thousand years. The English people were to build their houses of strange woods cut from many forests: from oak and from beech, from maple and pine, from teak and mahogany, from eucalyptus and redwood. They took with them

L

their language, their laws and their conception of government by consultation and consent. And men descended from the Celtic charioteers of Britain, from the Romans and their foreign legionaries who served in the northern island, from the Germanic warriors, from Danish and Norse seamen and rovers, from Norman landowner and Scandinavian farmer, live to this day in every continent outside Europe, and in every climate from the northern snows to the southern sun.

APPENDIX

THE FIRST POETRY

TACITUS records that the tribes of Germany recounted the deeds of their gods and heroes in verse. That the earliest poetry current among the ancestors of the English should have been narrative in form is what one would expect in a society where reading and writing were virtually unknown, and where the renown of ancient kings and the fame of ancestors, meant so much. Where stories had to be handed down verbally, poetry had obvious advantages over prose: the insistent rhythm, the set form, the rules governing the order and placing of words, all help the individual memory and make it possible to record long and complicated narratives.

None of the songs of the time of Tacitus has survived. But the Angles and Saxons brought the memory of such songs with them. Soon after they settled in Britain and once they had started to acquire the arts of reading and writing through their contact with the Christian world, the new English people began to write down old songs and to compose new ones. They retained the old forms but very early developed new and vastly richer themes.

These forms were strict and elaborate. Unlike the poetry of Greece and Rome, English verse relied upon the natural rhythms of the spoken language rather than upon specialised and arbitrarily selected rhythms. In Greek and in Latin each line in a poem had to have a fixed number of syllables, the number being fixed not by the needs of the sentence, but by the effect which the poem sought to make. Rules had been established very early and were followed almost without change for centuries. The Greek or Latin poet, according to whether he was telling the story of gods and heroes, recounting the sorrows and anguish of love, or composing a lyric, had to trim and organise his sentences to fit into the strictly predetermined number of syllables appropriate to any one line.

The rules followed by the first English poets were as firm and unchanging, but gave a great deal more flexibility. Each line had to be divided into two half-lines, separated by a pause. The first half-line usually included two syllables upon which emphasis would fall according to the normal rhythm and intonation of speech; the second half-line usually had one. All the stressed syllables in the line had to begin with the same sound: with the same letter if a consonant, or with any vowel. But the number of syllables in any line could vary, and the position of the stressed syllables was not fixed. The poet had at his command all the variety and subtleties of natural speech, decorated by alliteration but unfettered by syllabic counting.

Here, with the words modernised, are a few lines from *Beowulf*, the great epic poem of the first English. The passage describes a ship-funeral: King Scyld is laid by the mast of his ship which is then set on fire so that the dead king and his ship are cremated together.

There at the haven stood   the high-stemmed ship,
Icy and outward bound,   for the Atheling's faring;
They laid down then   the beloved chieftain,
The man by the mast.   There was many a treasure,
From far away,   fair treasures loaded.
Never heard I of comelier   keel so adorned
With warrior's weapons   and war armour,
Bills and byrnies.   On his breast they laid
Mighty treasures many,   that these might, with him
Into the flood's possession,   far depart. . . .
Then over him they set   a standard all golden,
High over his head;   they let the high seas bear him,

Sailing over the sea,   for him sad were their hearts,
Mournful their mood.   Men can never
Say in sooth,   men seated in hall
Heroes under heaven,   who this high load received.

Even in this modern dress the words give something of the sweep and rhythm of the original. The steady beat of the stressed words makes the poem apt for reciting or intoning to the plucked strings of a harp. The free form of the lines makes for a natural flow of words in the order and forms of everyday speech, with no tricks of inversion. Long after the forms and fashions of English poetry had been influenced by the Latin styles (first through contact with the French Normans and later by the Renaissance) this freedom and this simplicity of language remained and still remain its essential components. Shakespeare in *Love's Labour's Lost* writes with a Latin pen, but in the more nervous and sinewy language pattern of *The Tempest* and *King Lear* are echoes of the kind of poetry which the Angles and Saxons knew. Ordinary language and natural speech rhythms are enhanced not so much by the decorative value of the verse forms as by the strength and muscularity of the sentences and by the vivid quality of the content. It is what is said that transmutes simplicity into magic. The English poet who has his eyes fixed on the stars is in some danger of stumbling. If he keeps his eyes firmly on the land and on the sea he may well describe the starlight vividly and magically.

The earliest poem that has survived is *Widsith* which was written down some time in the seventh century, two hundred years after the English came to Britain and a mere fifty years or so after they received Christianity. It is evident that the growing literacy which the church brought to the English was quickly turned to purely secular purposes. For *Widsith* has little to do with Christianity and much to do with the already ancient traditions of celebrating in verse the memory of gods and heroes. It is in fact a catalogue of all the great ones of the earth as their names are remembered by an Englishman in the AD 600s, and Widsith the poet recounts how he was with them all. In his own person he thus symbolises all the poets who made immortal the names of their contemporary leaders, by celebrating their prowess in songs that lived on long after their armour had fallen to rust and their tombs had been overthrown. In his own person too he embodies the idea of poetic imagination. He does not merely remember the heroes of the past; he sees them in his mind's eye as a contemporary spectator.

Most of the leaders he mentions were the kings and heroes of the lands round the Baltic or on the shores of the North Sea. These were the homelands of the Angles and Saxons, and Widsith seems to be recording some of the old tales brought with them to Britain. He adds the names of others from far lands: the Israelites, of whom the new faith of Christianity had taught him; Alexander, 'greatest of all mankind'; Caesar, 'who ruled the Greeks'; the Syrians, the Medes, the Egyptians and others. But it is the northern heroes whose ghosts stalk most majestically through his mind and whose deeds he describes in detail. The legendary and terrible Attila appears as *Aetla*, ruler of the Huns; Eormanric, King of the Goths seventy years before the English came to Britain, Widsith still remembers as 'the fierce and faithless man'. Gefwulf, King of the Jutes, is recalled, and the mythical Wade, father of Weland the Smith whose name the English brought with them into Britain and who is still remembered there. (Among the upland fields of the Berkshire Downs there stands a neolithic stone-chambered tomb, already ancient when the English came. To this they attached the name of Weland, and it is known as Weland's Smithy to this day.) Widsith recalls too the names of great heroes who are also mentioned in other poems, such as King Offa of the Angles, who marked out the boundary of his kingdom 'with his single sword'.

There is one brief glimpse in the poem of the new legends which the English had learned in Britain and of the new thread of history now woven into their own tapestry : 'I was with Caesar who had feasting cities in his possession, wealth and lovely things and the kingdom of the Welsh'. By the time the poem was written, the Caesars had ceased to possess Britain, 'the kingdom of the Welsh', for more than two and a half centuries. But the memory of their presence had been preserved by the Britons and transmitted to the folklore of the English.

Widsith gains its effect through the sheer weight and length of the list of proper names, each of which would have evoked an heroic response in the minds of the listeners. It recounts but hardly comments upon human affairs. There is however another poem, *Deor*, in which a different poet speaks of ancient heroes and draws comfort from their tragedies and sorrows. Deor the poet has had taken from him the land that his patron, the King of the Heodings, had once given him. He is now poor, and has no lord and his sufferings seem endless. But he looks back to the sufferings of others, long since dead: their pains are over—so may his be:

Weland, he in Wermaland   wretchedness knew,
A stedfast man,   with sadness and hardship,
Had as companions still   sorrow and longing,
Winter-cold wretchedness;   woes often found,
Since on him Nithhad   need and force laid,
Supple sinew-bonds,   on so good a man—
    That passed over,   this may do so.

Theodric too is mentioned, as in Widsith:

Theodric ahte   thritig wintra
Maeringa burgh,   thaet waes monegum cuth,
    Thaes ofer-eode, thisses swa maeg.

Theodric governed,   thirty winters,
The Merovingian city,   that was to many known.
    That passed over,   this may do so!

King Eormanric, Widsith's 'fierce and faithless man', is remembered by Deor as a grim king:

We ge-ascodan   Eormanrices
Wylfenne ge-thoht.   Aht wide folc
Gotena rices. Thaet was grim cyning. . . .

We have asked about   Eormanric's
Wolfish thought.   He ruled a wide folk
Of the Gothic kingdom. That was a grim king!
Sat soldiers many,   by sorrow bound,
Woes awaiting,   wishing often
That this kingdom   overcome might be.
That passed over,   this may do so!

Deor might be called the first recorded English lyric. For in it the deeds of the dead kings, the sufferings of the vanished heroes and the oppression endured by the subjects of tyrants are not the sole topic. They are used partly perhaps because no audience of the period would find any poem acceptable that was not concerned with gods or heroes; and partly because the poet himself knew no other way. But they are entirely subordinated to the purely lyric theme of the poet's own sorrow and the comfort he finds in the transience of all mortal things, including pain. It is not Weland's sorrow we remember but the desolation of Deor the poet. And he has imposed a lyrical shape upon the old heroic narrative form, by his use of the refrain, simple, natural, and deeply moving in its haunting and magical repetition.

The theme that all mortal things shall perish is a recurrent one. Shakespeare was not the first to state starkly that 'the cloud-capped towers, the gorgeous palaces, yea the earth itself and all that it inherits shall dissolve'. In a poem known as *The Ruin* an Anglo-Saxon poet surveys a deserted Roman city and meditates upon the decayed splendour of the buildings, the homes of rulers and warriors now dead. The invading English were not entering a waste land or a wilderness of virgin forest and heath. The Roman roads still stretched across the countryside and the Roman cities still stood, though derelict and falling into final ruin. At every turn the Anglo-Saxon traveller would have seen, as did the writer of this poem, the 'wonderful stonework, the fortifications decayed, the roofs fallen, the towers in ruins . . .' The poet saw in his mind's eye the days of the city's splendour. The castle rooms had been bright and many were the baths there. There had been many mead-halls full of joyful men. Men light of heart and bright with gold, splendidly adorned, proud and filled with wine, shone in their battle-armour, and looked about them on treasure, on silver and fine jewels, on riches and on possessions, on the bright cattle of this wide kingdom.

This is not the voice of a barbarian looking with uncomprehending awe upon the ruins of an ancient civilisation, from which not only time but his own ignorance divides him. A civilised and compassionate man is seeing among the dead stone and broken tiles the proud ghosts of those who walked the earth before him. His imagination is the begetter of his compassion, and his compassion gives new depth to his imagination. Poetry is no longer a mere list of heroes, nor a tale of some ancient and well-known adventure. Like *Deor*, this poem is truly lyrical, but it has departed even further than *Deor* from the conventions of the past. *Deor*'s personal commentary, moving though it be, is no more than a commentary upon the well-known and well-worn theme of ancient heroes. In *The Ruin* there are no known heroes; the ghosts who people the dead city are created by the poet, who evokes the past within himself. His own thoughts are not merely a commentary, but the whole theme.

Perhaps it is because the rhythms and patterns of English poetry are those of ordinary speech, that something of the poet's personality and attitudes, can be felt across the dividing centuries. We are not merely told of the strange land of Britain, lying in the twilight between the sunset of Rome and the dawn of England, a green land crossed by great roads and scattered with deserted cities, where shops and baths, public buildings and private dwellings, lay hushed in the northern sunshine : we see all this through the eyes of the new inhabitants. The latter had learned from the Britons, whose lands they were occupying, tales of the old days when the cities had been crowded and prosperous. Yet still they saw them as something mysterious, and the poet speaks of the ruined walls as 'the work of giants'.

Much about the first English can be learned from other poems. Tacitus's description of how men looked to their chief for equipment and treasure is recalled by poem after poem. In *Beowulf*,

M

King Scyld is called *beaga bryttan,* the bestower of rings. Another passage describes the presents from King Hrothgar, 'the giver of treasure', to Beowulf and his companions. Eight horses with golden bridles were led into the hall. One bore a great ornamental saddle, the king's own war-seat. These horses, with a fine helmet and a chain-mail corselet or byrnie, he gave to Beowulf, as well as a golden battle ensign. Here the English are remembering in their new home a custom they had followed centuries before.

Even when kings and emperors of other nations were celebrated, the Anglo-Saxon poets conceived them as kings of their own kind. In the poem *Elene,* which describes the discovery of the True Cross by Helena, mother of Constantine, the latter—though a Roman Emperor—is still called 'the protector of the soldiers, the giver of rings to men'. And loyalty to a lord was not an abstract conception; it was made up partly of gratitude for gifts of treasure and of beer and mead. *Finnesburgh* is a poem which describes a bitter five-day battle for possession of the hall of a young king. In the dark of night and in the changing light of the moon the attack begins. The young king's sixty warriors fight stoutly for their lord. 'I have never heard,' exclaims the poet, 'of sixty brave warriors bearing themselves better, more bravely in a battle of men, nor of young men giving better service in return for the sweet mead that the king had given to his men'.

The loss of a lord was a great sorrow and a masterless man was a thing of pity. *The Wanderer* describes the sorrows of a man whose lord is dead and who vainly seeks another protector.

Often he who's alone,   prays for honour and protection,
Mercy of Mighty God.   Though his mood is of care,
He rows with his hands   on the rime-cold sea,
Woeful and wretched,   his weird is fully set.

A man's 'weird' was his fate, the destiny which he could not escape. This fatalism is pre-Christian in origin, and it renders prayer useless and takes no cognisance of the mercy of God.

Shakespeare's three weird sisters are the three fates of the Graeco-Roman world, as half-understood and dimly remembered by the first English. Something of this pagan fatalism still survives among the English people, particularly in stress of war or danger. Later, the poem reverts to the same theme :

Ne maeg werig mod   wyrde withstondan. . . .

Nor may the weary mood   its weird withstand

And the wanderer seeks everywhere a new lord and a new protector :

Where I, far or near,   might ever find one
Who in the mead-hall   myself would know
Or be a friend to me,   fairly comfort me. . . .

He remembers the past in his dreams. The loss of his lord evokes a mood that modern minds find difficult to understand, and would associate more with the loss of a lover :

When sorrow and sleep   sweep up together on
The poor man, alone,   and often bind him,
He thinks in his mind   that he his lord of men
Clasps and kisses,   on his kind knee laying
Hand and head   as in happier days.

But there is only winter-care and the cold sea.

The sea itself is the theme of another poem known as *The Seafarer*. It gives no romantic picture of the wide waters, telling of the cold, the hardship and the danger and of the cries of wild birds; but it speaks clearly of the strange and abiding relationship that has always existed between the Anglo-Saxons and the sea. To the later Roman writers the Saxons appeared at home on water and heedless of its danger. But the Romans could not see into the hearts of the sailors (whither this poem so directly takes us) nor understand that to the Saxons the sea has always been the cruel sea, harsh and unforgiving, yet always fascinating and always to be challenged.

The poem speaks of the

> dwellings in the ships. Dreadful was the wave's movement. Hard waking at night by the ship's prow was often my work, when the ship rolled near the cliffs. I was chilled with the cold, my feet fettered by the frost, with cold bands. . . . The hail was flying. There was no noise but the seas breaking, the ice-cold billows, or the song of the swans. My gladness was in the gannet's cry and the curlew, not in men's laughter; in the gull's mewing, not in drinking the mead. . . . The darkness of night grew deep, and snow came from the north and frost bound the earth firmly. Hail scattered on the ground, like cold grains of corn.

And then, through all his hardships, he thinks of the sweet land and its beauties : 'The woods have their flowers, the towns are lovely and the fields are fair'.

Some time in the AD 700s, a hundred years after the English had adopted Christianity, a poet rewrote the Book of Genesis as a poem. Probably a monk working in the north, he brought much of the older poetic conventions of phrase and language to his task. The King of Sodom and Gomorrah is 'their loved giver of gold, their companion in battle'. It is a faithful enough rendering of the story, but the style is not outstanding, nor does the poem have the ring of a personal voice. About a hundred years later another English poet translated another version of Genesis which had been written by one of the Old Saxons, that is to say by one of those who were still living in their original German homeland. This poem, *Genesis B*, is a remarkable work. The fall of Lucifer and his brave defiance of God are the main themes and the sympathy of the writer is, for all his pious devotion, clearly with the fallen angel who has the courage and resolution to face certain defeat at the hands of the omnipotent power of God. The poem breathes the spirit that animated the Anglo-Saxons at war, for whom defiance of odds, and an obstinate willingness to fight a hopeless fight, meant so much. And it anticipates Milton by seven hundred years. It brings home how continuous is the stream of English poetry and how ancient is the spirit that inspired the rebellious and defeated

Milton, blind and helpless, to cry out with Satan : 'What though the field be lost? All is not lost!' In *Genesis B* the tale is told thus :

Then had the All-Ruler,   of the angels' host,
(Through His hand's might),   the Holy Lord,
Ten Tribes set up,   whom he trusted well,
That they would be faithful,   and follow him truly,
Working his will.   Therefore wits he gave them,
And with his hands shaped them,   the Holy Lord.
He had set them in splendour;   one he had most strongly made,
So mighty in his mind's thought.   He let him rule much,
Highest under Him in Heaven's kingdom.   He had made him
wholly white,
So bright was his beauty in Heaven, that had come to him from
the Lord of Battles.
He was like to the light of the stars.   He was to love the Lord's
work
Great was to be his gaiety in heaven,   he was to give God
thanks.

But this bright angel grew proud and impatient of serving One greater than himself :

He said that his body was   bright and shining,
White and in hue most bright;   nor could he in his heart find it
That he to God should   give the goodness of faith,
Thus to serve the Lord thoroughly;   thought he by himself
That he of might and craft,   the more had
Than Holy God   might have himself,
The mighty one!   Many words he spoke
This angel so over-proud;   he thought, through his own craft,
How he should there set up   a throne more mighty,
Higher in Heaven.   He said his heart moved him
That he west and north   to work should begin.
He built a great building; said that doubt beset him,
Whether he should be God's own   good disciple!
'What shall I win here?' said he.   'I need no wiser master,
Nor to have one higher.   With my own hands many
Wonders I'll work,   (I've wielded much power)
To get for myself   a goodlier throne,
Higher in Heaven.   Why should I serve this high Master,

Bow to him in goodness?   I may be a God as he is!
Now stand by me, strong warriors,   who will not in the strife
                                                        fail me;
High in courage, hard-minded,   they have chosen me as the
                                                        highest,
Brave ones about me.   With such may a man think out the
                                                        brightest of plans!
I keep such companions.   Their friendship is keenest.
They hold their hearts fast.   I may be the highest among them,
And so keep a kingdom.   I count it not right
That I ever should need   again to flatter
God to seek any good.   Nor will I give him my homage!'

After the angel's defiance, God cast him out of heaven into
a place of fire and of great cold, where there were flames and
where nevertheless there was darkness. But even in his torment,
and after God had rebuked him, Satan speaks again. He in turn
rebukes God for casting him out with no sin proved against
him.

. . . .   This is my greatest sorrow
That Adam shall,   who from earth was made,
Now seek to hold   my splendid throne,
Wide joys winning, while woes I suffer,
And all harms in this hell! Ah now, if I had my hands' power,
And could, for one moment,   go out once more,
For one winter-hour,   then I with these warriors—

Just as the kings of other lands were seen by the English poets
as kings after the English fashion, so Satan is seen as one of their
own warriors, defeated but unyielding, determined to fight with
whatever weapons are available. Satan is a figure deserving
neither anger nor contempt, but compelling admiration and
pity.

One of the latest poems is perhaps one of the greatest. In
AD 991, Byrhtnoth, an Earl in Essex and a leader under King
Aethelred, fought a battle against the Danes and died in the
fighting. The events are recorded in a long poem, *The Battle
of Maldon*, which contains almost all that we need to know

about the Anglo-Saxon attitudes to war, to loyalty, to resolution, and to defeat.

The poem as we have it (for the beginning of the text is lost) opens with the imminence of battle. Some of Byrhtnoth's men had ridden to the field on horseback.

Loud ordered he his levies   to leave their horses,
Far to drive them   and forth to go,
Giving heed to their hands   and their heart's courage.
And then Offa his kinsman   at once found
That Byrhtnoth would not   brook any slackness.
Then let he from his hand   his beloved hawk
Fly to the woods   and he to the war stepped.
By this a man might know   that this knight would never
Wax weak at the war,   when his weapons he took.

The quality of vivid physical description is here well exemplified, the hush before battle caught for all time, without any use of metaphor or symbolism, or any heightening of language. Byrhtnoth draws up his men and gives them their orders. The Danes, over the river, first offer to depart in peace if they are given gold. Byrhtnoth defies them : the only treasure they will receive will be deadly spears and ancient swords. In the battle that follows, Byrhtnoth is killed, and his men fight on, remembering the boasts they had made in happier days that they would support their lord and never survive him in battle. The English defeat was total and it is a defeat which the poet chooses to celebrate, together with those qualities of desperate bravery which it brought forth. The poem is immensely moving because of its complete realism and simple narrative.

Some years earlier, in AD 937, another battle had been fought, at Brunnanburgh in the north. King Aethelstan of Wessex with his brother Edmund, had fought a mixed army of Scots and Norsemen and had defeated them. The entry in the *Anglo-Saxon Chronicle* takes the form of seventy-three lines of poetry :

Here Aethelstan the King,   of Earls the lord
Bestower of rings,   and his brother also,

Edmund the Aetheling,   everlasting fame
Beat out in battle,   with the broad sword's edge.

The poet does not describe the battle itself but the appearance
of the field in the cold dawn, when the fighting was over. The
sun rose, 'God's bright candle'; the mangled dead, Scots and
Norsemen, lay lifeless. Five kings were slain that day, and seven
earls from among the Norsemen who sailed away to Dublin.
The birds of prey and the wild beasts moved in for their feast
of flesh. There came the black ravens with their horny beaks and
the grey-coated eagles with their white tails, and the greedy
hawk:

> . . . . *ond thaet graege deor*
> *Wulf on wealde. . . .*

> . . . . and that grey beast
> The wolf of the weald . . .

Again it is the simplicity of the description, the lack of orna-
ment, that makes the scene live. Because there were Scots among
the enemy, the poet is reminded of the early battles which his
ancestors had fought five hundred years ago. The memory of
the invasion still lived. For there never was greater slaughter,
he writes—

> . . . . *sythen eastan hider*
> *Engle ond Seaxe   up becomen*
> *Ofer brad brimu,   Brytene sohton,*
> *Wlance wigsmithas   Wealas ofercomon,*
> *Eorlas arhwate   eard begeaton.*

> . . . . since from the east hither
> Angles and Saxon   up did come,
> Over the broad sea's brim,   Britain they sought
> Wise warsmiths;   the Welsh overcoming
> Earls fame-loving,   the earth they seized.

The poet's version of how the Angles and Saxons overcame

the Welsh recalls that English kings in fact allied themselves with kings of the Britons to fight rival English kings; and
Britons continued to live on in the English kingdoms, as far east
as Kent, as the laws reveal. Something of the customs and
culture of the Britons was transferred to the new masters of the
land and had its effect upon the poetry. There is even evidence
that the British method of brewing beer not only survived in
England but was held in high esteem! It is true that the Britons
did not quickly share their learning and their Christian religion
with the invaders. This indeed was one of Augustine's chief
complaints against them. But it is inconceivable that the customs
of the older folk left the newer unaffected.

The poetry of the later Britons is well documented and fairly
extensive. Known to us as early Welsh poetry it is in striking
contrast to the English poetry at which we have glanced. The
Britons had been literate for a long while, and their poetry was
more sophisticated, more learned and richer in tradition than
the English counterpart. The form is stricter and more formal.
The language is a specialised language with hyperbole and exag-
geration. Where in early English poetry men fight hand-to-hand
and one kills another and the spears fly, in Welsh poetry a man's
prowess is described rather than his actual feats of war. Of
Arthur's companion Kay a poem in *The Black Book of
Carmarthen* says:

His vengeance was mighty.
He was to be feared in battle.
When he drank from the drinking horn
He drank as much as four men.
When he went to the wars,
He slaughtered as a hundred men would slay.
Without God's own will
Kay's death could not be effected.

Here is no stark realism, the bite of sword-edge, the sweat of
battle. Here rather is imagination taking flight from things of
the earth into quite another region. In another poem, *Culhwch*

and Olwen, the hero's battle axe 'would draw blood from the wind. It could fall more swiftly than a dewdrop falling from a leaf to the ground'. He rides so lightly that nothing stirs beneath the hooves of his horse. But the horse conjures up no such real picture as do the steeds of Byrhtnoth's men, driven far off before the riders step into the fight. Men are described by elliptical and brief epithets. *The Black Book* describes the gatekeeper of a castle as 'Glewlwyd of the fierce grip', and Manawyddan son of Llyr as 'wise in counsel'. True, the Anglo-Saxon poets also had their conventional adjectives. But such is their interest in the outer and visible world that there breaks through, from time to time, a vivid glimpse of the world they saw, the rough sea, the cold hail, the hard beaks of the ravens, or the broken walls of a derelict city. For the Britons the real world faded when poetry came upon them, and another dream-world was superimposed upon it.

In this other world numbers were important and became a part of the magical pattern. Culhwch, denied entrance to a castle, threatens to give 'three shouts at the entrance'. Why three? The thought would not have occurred to a poet of the first English. Moreover he says that his shouts will be heard on a hilltop in Cornwall, in the north country, and over in Ireland : even the hyperbole is set into the pattern of three. Kay slew his enemies 'three at a time'—a statement that would have struck a commonsensical Saxon poet as nonsense. Moreover the foe fell a hundred at a time before Bedevere. Then again, Kay slew nine witches (three times three). The Britons indeed wrote a whole series of poems listing events, heroes or places in groups of three. And within the pattern of three, other numbers are set. Among these poems (the *Triads*) there is one describing the three great choirs in Britain and 'in each there were 2,400 holy men, that is there were a hundred for every hour, day and night'.

The other world lies over and obscures the world of reality. Kay goes to the Isle of Mona to slay lions, though all—poet and audience alike—knew that there were no lions there. A man could be mortally wounded yet live and jest. When Culhwch thrusts a spear through the eye of an enemy, so that it protrudes through the back of his neck, the foeman merely says that in future the wind will make his eyes water and his eyesight will be the poorer. Kings are turned into wild boars. Men are sent on strange quests for a magic cauldron or set to clear a great wood and plough the land, all in a day. As an illustration of the carrying-over of the legends of the Britons into the lands of the English, a late medieval English poet in the north wrote down, in good alliterative verse, the old British tale of *Sir Gawaine and the Green Knight*. The form was English. But the magic belt, the quest of other-world adventures, the Green Knight, after decapitation, holding his head while it speaks to his assailant— all this is pure Briton.

There are two kinds of imagination : the ability to see in the mind's eye a clear and accurate image of the world about us, and in our library or workroom to hold the image of an eagle's white tail or the hard grain of the hail; and there is also the ability to make images in the mind that are changing and flickering pictures of the world, transmitted into magic by our own psychological needs, through symbolism, hyperbole and the wild logic of dreams.

English poetry, by great good fortune, is the inheritor of both. Yet in it there is perhaps a slight emphasis on the first kind of imagination, that records the colour of a daisy, the texture of grass, the voices and sinews of real men in a workaday but none the less heroic world.

INDEX